Secret Healing of Mental Illness at Chottanikkara Devi Temple, Kerala

Authors

Chittaranjan Subudhi
Soumya S B
Edness Rutta

Indian Society of Professional Social Work (ISPSW)

Secret Healing of Mental Illness at Chottanikkara Devi Temple, Kerala

Author(s):

Chittaranjan Subudhi, Soumya S B, Edness Rutta

Publisher: Indian Society of Professional Social Work (ISPSW)
Registered office: Department of Psychiatric Social Work,
NIMHANS, Bangalore - 5600029
Secretariat: Mental Health Institute (MHI)
(Adjoining Punjab Police Institute)
Sector 32 C, Chandigarh – 160030
Email ID: contact.ispsw@gmail.com
Website: www.ispsw.net

ISBN: 978-81-954684-0-9

Dedication

Dedicated to the People with Mental Illness

Acknowledgment

Attempting to write a book is like embarking on a journey through unknown seas. The work was the long pending work stated as a master's degree thesis, and after a long effort, it came to its final shape.

It's a great pleasure following the successful completion of an important task that would have remained incomplete without a word of gratitude to all those who made an incredible dream to a reality. We are humbled and grateful to express our sincere appreciation to those who provided us with support and encouragement. We express our special thanks to the research participants who allowed us into their lives and experiences.

First and foremost, we praise and thank the Almighty God for giving us strength and blessings so we could go this far and manage to accomplish this book.

Apart from him, we are incredibly thankful to the Central University of Tamil Nadu administration and the Department of Social Work for the opportunity to conduct this study.

Sincere appreciation is extended to Kochin Devasom trustee members and all friends, family members, teachers, colleagues, and students for their encouragement and support throughout this assignment.

Sincerely we thank everyone who helped during this study and completion of the book.

Chittaranjan Subudhi
Soumya SB
Edness Rutta

Contents

List of Tables

List of Figures

PREFACE

Mental illness is a disorder that affects mood, thinking, and behavior. Recently high prevalence has been marked all over the world. In middle and low-income countries, more than 80 percent of people with mental illnesses do not receive proper treatment for various reasons. Some reasons are poor understanding of mental illness, inaccessibility of services, and scarcity of mental experts in hospitals.

India marks a high rate of the prevalence of mental illness. It is among the countries overburdened with poor understanding of mental illness and inaccessibility of services, especially in rural areas where most people with mental illness reside. Inaccessibility of mental health services, poverty, and scarcity of mental health are among the hindrances in seeking proper medication; people's attachment to the disease with evil spirits affects much adequate attendance of treatment. The paper intends to understand the models and the experiences of the family and people with mental illness at the Chottanikkara temple.

In exploring the general understanding of models and experiences of the affected, the study had the following objectives: (1) to explore the explanatory models of mental illness among patients with mental illness and their family members who are attending the Chottanikkara Devi temple for healing; (2) to explore the patients and their family member's experiences of temple healing at Chottanikkara Devi temple; and (3) to document the healing process adopted by the Chottanikkara Devi temple.

The study was conducted in Chottanikkara Temple in Kerala, where the purposive sampling technique was used to obtain 14 participants. The target population were people with mental illness and their family members who attended the Chottanikkara temple for healing. The qualitative approach was used to conduct in-depth interviews to achieve the intended study objectives.

The study found that a majority of patients with mental illness strongly believed that their illness was just a possession of evil spirits and had nothing to do with mental issues. With such belief, they concluded that the perfect cure for the disease is through temple healing. A few patients knew of mental health problems. They sought medical assistance, but due to their inability to afford the medical expenses, medication challenges, and slight improvement, they opted for temple healing. The use of different specified rituals in assisting people with mental illness improved the situation of the patients, as explained. However, some reported that they are felling better at the time of staying around the temple; but when they return home, the illness begins.

The study recommends awareness building on mental health issues should be accelerated extensively since the situation of mental illness is escalating for various reasons. Any person can be subjected to mental health issues; hence proper understanding and awareness of the disease and available facilities to assist the needy. This will improve the ability to seek help early in the problem.

CHAPTER I

BACKGROUND

Mental illnesses are significant worldly concerns due to their gradual increase (WHO, 2001). The escalation rate pushed national and international organizations to include mental health policies as a priority and part of the sustainable Development Goals. Mental health is an inseparable component of health; maintaining it helps to stabilize behavior, emotions, and thoughts. World Health Organization (WHO, 2014) stated that 'there is no health without mental health.' "It is a state of well-being in which an individual realizes their abilities to cope with the normal life stress, can work productively, enhance self-image and improve relationships which holistically improve the standard of living and productivity quality of life to an individual, family, and society at large" (WHO, 2014).

Mental health problems are common in all societies and significantly contribute to the burden of diseases (Pathak & Subudhi, 2020). The high prevalence are marked in developed and developing countries, which calls for effective interventions in dealing with the issue. Globally, more than 450 million people have any form of mental disorder (WHO, 2001). Currently, mental and behavioral disorders account for about 12% of the global burden of diseases, which may increase to 15% (WHO, 2001). The environment and biological predisposition are the significant causes of mental health problems and create many daily life problems.

Even though the seriousness of the disease in low and middle-income countries, between 76% and 85% of people with mental illnesses receives no treatment for their disorders (Wang et al., 2007). Mental illnesses can be cured or managed with the recent medical advancement, yet the gap between people needing care and those who access it remains substantial (WHO, 2019a). World Health Report (2006) highlighted the shortage of health workers in low and middle-income countries. The scarcity of human resources in these countries led to a lack of services, especially in rural areas. In Africa, the average rate of psychiatric is 0.05/100,000 population, While Europe is 9/100,000 population, and India's ratio is 0.3/100,000, with about 7.5% of its people struggling with mental health issues (WHO, 2019b). Despite the seriousness of the situation, the attention and resources devoted to mental health services are inadequate.

Studies show that mental illnesses have a long history, traced from the second millennium B.C (Kyziridis, 2005). The ancient Egyptian book of hearts, the Hindu, and the early Chinese scriptures had descriptions of mental illnesses and their remedies. In ancient times, almost all societies attached the disease to spiritual causes.

Mental illness is a significant area affected by religious beliefs, culture, and traditions that hinder effective medical interventions. Cultural diversity plays a vital role in how people view and act on different issues in worldwide. Likewise, the definition of mental illness is reflected differently across the globe. People's understanding, perceptions, health-seeking behavior, and attitudes are all affected by their cultural practices and beliefs (Hernandez et al., 2009). Culture defines a problem, how the problem is understood and how to resolve the issue. Due to cultural beliefs and customs, mental illness is perceived differently across cultures.

Current research shows that researchers have increasingly sought to understand the relationship between mental illness and spirituality over the past few years. Since the disease has been associated with spirituality, people seem to be reluctant to accept medical assistance (Hernandez et al., 2009; Biswal et al., 2017; Bhattacharya, 1954). Religious healing or spiritual power in healing is the belief in the presence of supernatural powers, which can restore the natural order miraculously. The healing process can be done in many forms, such as by performing prayers and other rituals (Vallenga, 2008). Different religions deploy different modalities in performing healing rituals.

India is among the countries with a high prevalence of mental illness and is severely understaffed (WHO, 2019a). The National Mental Health Survey 2016 reported that 14% of India's population requires active mental health intervention. In dealing with the problem, the Government of India launched the National Mental Health Program (NMHP) in 1982 and strengthened it by implementing the District Mental Health Programme (DMHP) in 1996. All these are aimed at improving the mental health services in the country. Despite the efforts made, India still marked being understaffed (Subudhi, 2021).

The country has been marking excellent economic growth recently though very few resources, but the resources allocated in the health sector are still inadequate to reduce the challenges. The allocation is a little over 1% of the country's GDP. Such low allocation of resources affects the quality of services (Sanjay, 2018). Apart from that, other challenges associated are people's strong attachment to beliefs, lack of awareness, difficulty in accessibility, availability, and affordability of medical services for people with mental illnesses. The low income is also becoming increasingly prohibitive for them to access quality medical services.

There is a dare need for governments and non-governmental organizations to assist policymakers, health planners, and educators in addressing the shortfall in human resources for mental health care. Some non-governmental organizations and civil society groups are trying to provide mental health services through daycare centers, halfway homes, long-stay homes, counseling centers, suicide prevention centers, and school mental health programs. Most of the programs are found in urban areas in various places, with little consideration for rural areas. The study aims to find the models and the experiences of the family and people with mental health conditions at Chottanikkara temple and develop an intervention to change the existing perception since the present perception decelerates the means of dealing with mental issues, which are growing, steadily with the development of science and technology.

Culture, Religion, and Mental Illness

Culture is one of the essential concepts in social science. Culture is a broad term that includes all our lifestyles, modes of behavior, ethics, morals, manners, customs, traditions, and religious activity. Cultural traits and norms shape our normative behavior practices and beliefs, influence our thinking and define our everyday activities (Satcher, 2001). Culture plays a vital role in explaining mental illness because different people have their own cultural beliefs to find the causes of mental illness, treatment, and intervention. People's perceptions and explanations of mental illness are shaped by the culture they belong to (Hernandez et al., 2009).

Religious healing or spiritual power in recovery is the belief in the presence of supernatural powers, which can restore the natural order miraculously. The healing can be done in many forms, such as by performing prayers and other rituals (Vallenga, 2008). Different religions or belief systems deploy different modalities in performing healing rituals.

Cultural diversity worldwide affects how people view and act on different issues. Likewise, the definition of mental illness is viewed differently in different parts of the world. People's understanding, perceptions, health-seeking behavior, and attitudes are all affected by their cultural practices and beliefs (Hernandez et al., 2009). Culture defines a problem, how the problem is understood and how to resolve the issue.

Traditional African countries perceive mental illness due to ancestors, misfortunes, and bewitchment by evil spirits. In addition, traditional healers or religious leaders are believed to possess the power to resolve the issue (Ngubane, 1977). In Southern Asia and other Islamic countries, Jinn is often associated with mental illness; Evil eyes from envy can result in other personal misfortunes (Dein & Illaiee, 2013). In India, mental illnesses are perceived to result from violated vows, promises or deeds, possession of spirits, sexual overindulgence, disrespect to Gods, and violation of social taboos (Weiss et al., 1986). Glick (1967) has mentioned that "it is common knowledge that ideas and practices relating to the illness are inseparable from the domain of religious beliefs and practices in many cultures."

Why do people seek spiritual healing?

General understanding of the illness determines whether people are motivated to seek treatment; how they cope with the symptoms, family support, and where they seek help (USDHHS, 2001). Mental illness perception and etiology have differed across cultures (Biswal et al., 2021; Hernandez et al., 2009). This explains the view of illness causality at an individual level or situated in the natural or social world, and each society views these differently. Some described mental illnesses as a result of the evil spirit, black magic, or breaking of taboos. Religion and culture play an essential role in these perceptions, affecting the general healing process (Helman, 2007).

Association of mental illness with evil spirits resides today in some societies, which acts as a barrier for people to seek medical treatment. Communities that are still characterized by solid cultural beliefs lead to less use of pharmaceutical medicines (Helman, 2007).

According to the nature of the disease and its symptoms, people with mental illness face severe human rights violations, discrimination, and stigma, which hinder seeking professional assistance (Hampton & Sharp, 2014; Nguyen & Bernheimer, 2014). Shame, disgrace, and disapproval result in individual rejection and exclusion from participating in other social issues (WHO, 2001).

Furthermore, the nature and people's perception on the issue of mental illness lead to denial of fear of societal judgment and stigma. The issue of stigma is experienced in all countries, including developed and underdeveloped. Fear of stigma affects the treatment-seeking behavior among the population. In developed countries, due to that fear, people tend to seek assistance at the very acute stage of the disease (USDHHS, 2001).

Moreover, mental illness treatment-seeking is affected by interdependency in the family, community, and national systems (Helman, 2007; Hampton & Sharp, 2014). In low and middle-income families, social bonds and family are the safety nets of an individual. People with mental illnesses depend on their families for assistance. Hence, the family decides the level of care and the type of treatment. In places where the government safety net is minimal or does not exist, a lack of family support leads to the total neglect of the person.

Racism and Discrimination

In societies with a strong feeling of superiority and inferiority complex, people's classes affect seeking pharmaceutical assistance (Kumar & Subudhi, 2015). The inferior classes experience social alienation and stereotypes in accessing pharmaceutical aid, forcing them to seek assistance elsewhere (Fiske, 2017). Helping people with mental illnesses in recovery by facilitating their autonomy and assisting them to live and grow beyond limitations imposed by their condition can help their recovery. A sense of acceptance is vital in improving their mental abilities (Sadock et al., 2007). The upper-class people showed reorganization about the causes of illness. Kakar (1991), higher caste people showed greater reorganization of natural causes of illness, while lower caste believed more in witchcraft and other spiritual concepts. Educational factors, caste, social class, religious affiliation, and religious attendance affect psychiatric care-seeking.

Major Factors Hindering Medical Service Seeking in India

The reviews found that several reasons determine people's readiness to seek assistance for mental health issues. The major ones are strong cultural and religious beliefs—the level of discrimination and stigma associated with the illness, and the general understanding of mental illness issues. Racism and bigotry also affect services. The existing literature reveals that these are the factors affecting the determination of help-seeking from religious points, are (i) strong beliefs on supernatural etiology; (ii) easy access; (iii) influence and suggestions from relatives and community members; (iv) Stigma in consulting psychiatrists; (v) lack of mental health care resources of ; (vi) lack of knowledge about the onset of the illness; (Raghuram et al., 2002;

Padmavati et al., 2005; Sethi et al., 1977; Trivedi & Sethi, 1979; Satija et al., 1981).

Traditional cum religious healing in India

In India majority of its citizens embrace extreme cultural, traditions, and religious beliefs. To a certain extent, such strong beliefs are barriers to seeking professional assistance. In reforming the Indian psychiatrist from 1970 to the 1980s, mental health experts questioned the traditional healing world (Kakar, 1985; Subudhi et al., 2020). Since the Ervadi tragedy in 2001 marked a shift in the healing practices. The incident proved strong beliefs associated with the disease; caregivers flock to faith-based facilities to find a cure. The government prohibited the confinement of people with mental illnesses in unlicensed places (Subudhi, 2014).

Indian psychiatry is one of the differences. Its traditional understanding of mental health disorders as part of Ayurveda for the care of mentally ill patients. The principles of Ayurveda medicine on mental illness were developed long years back before Christ (Dube et al., 1984). The training procedure, ethical codes, metaphysical theories, and psychiatric treatments brought the attention of mental health experts. The current development of Yoga and meditation in improving mental health brings about new insights into dealing with mental issues. All of these show the contribution of Indian temple healing to help deal with mental issues (Murthy, 2011).

Healing intends to relieve pain, restore damage or deterioration, or assist a person from improper functioning (Alter, 1999). Though biomedical medicine has dominated the health care system in providing evidence-based treatment, traditional healing practices play a significant role and are widely accepted among the majority of the population over the globe (Samuel, 2015). Both social and cultural constructs play an essential role in understanding the subjective meaning of healing and its process.

According to Campion and Bhugra (1997), 45% of the patient presenting to a modern westernized psychiatric facility had seen religious healers before seeking help from a psychiatrist. In our society, one kind of stereotyped action is there. The people first visit the indigenous practices to heal their illness, and people have their explanations about their condition based on their traditional techniques and belief system. Religious prayers and healers play an essential role in treating illnesses, including mental illness. People gave priority to conventional or indigenous medical practitioners who may be living in rural or urban areas.

On the other hand, friends and relatives play a crucial role in referral to religious institutions. The people hide their illness and then secretly visit the faith healers of indigenous healers. Remove the myths and misconceptions about mental illness and sensitize the people to resources available in the community.

According to Benmebarek (2017), epidemiological studies across different nations show, that only about one-third of people with a mental disorder consult mental health services in Algeria. Others seek help from different sectors, such as family physicians, general practitioners, or other physicians, depending on the type of health system of the country. In high-income countries such as the USA, Canada, Italy, and the Netherlands, many patients with mental health problems never seek mental health assistance rather than the general health sector. In India, mental health services are still insufficient compared to high-income countries. According to a recent estimate, the country has just 0.25 psychiatric beds per 10000 population, 0.2 psychiatrists, 0.03 clinical psychologists, 0.05 psychiatric nurses, and 0.03 social workers per 10000 population. Psychiatric treatment facilities are available in psychiatric hospitals, general hospitals, psychiatric units, and office-based practices. As well as these patients depending on availability and accessibility, may consult non-psychiatric physicians, general practitioners, para-counselors, local religious healers, traditional healers, etc.

In India, many people troubled by emotional distress and severe mental illness go to Hindu, Christian, Muslim, and other religious centers for healing. In the country, people with mental illness mainly consult faith healers, folk heals, and indigenous medicine. Because they believe that mental illness do supernatural forces exercise the result of malicious influence by being alive or dead. Some temples are famous for the treatment of various diseases, especially mental illnesses. The temple has been used as a place of healing for incubation or temple sleep.

The majority of the illiterate people believed that God's blessing and temples built in his name have the power to heal mentally ill patients. So they were taken to those temples to be healed. About 80% of the rural population first consults faith healers. It is conceivable that temple priests or faith came from the same culture. "Demon or disorder" article states that religion is often the first contact with a person with mental illness (Stanford, 2007). The person seeks counsel from their religious counselor. Due to this inclination towards religion, a spiritual leader must be educated on mental illness with the freedom to translate it into their religious doctrine. Reciprocally, so should a mental health professional be aware of the religious or spiritual beliefs of the client and feel comfortable discussing interpretations of mental health symptoms through the lens of the client's beliefs (Miller, 1990). Working as an integrated team can increase the likelihood of positive outcomes.

Famous Temples for Healing Mental Illness in India

Muthusamy **Temple in Tamil Nadu:** The temple has situated in the village of Velayutham palayampudur, Dindugal District, Tamil Nadu. Set in the foothills of the Palani range of the Western Ghats. The temple was built 60 years back in the middle of the graveyard over the cemetery of Muthuswamy. A man who lived in that village about a century ago. During his lifetime, Muthuswamy was considered a strange person who worked little and spent his time wandering about in that village. According to local legend, towards the end of his life, people noticed that a mere touch of his hand cured many ailments, especially mental illnesses, and stories spread about his healing powers. After he passed away, the villagers built the temple over his grave, and it began to attract people with serious mental illnesses for their healing free of services (Raguram et al., 2002).

Agora Veerabhadra Swamy **Temple in Tamil Nadu:** Agora Veerabhadra Swamy Temple is in Hanumanthapuram Village near Chengalpattu in the Kanchipuram District of Tamil Nadu. Sri Agora Veerabhadra Swamy and Goddess Sri Kaalikaambal are the main deities of this temple. Many devotees gather and offer the pooja, especially on the day of the new moon and full moon. As per the legend, it is believed that people with mental illness are cured if they visit the deity of this temple. Many people with mental illness are brought here, and prayers are offered near Sri Agora Veerabadhrar. It is believed that Sri Agora Veerabadhrar blesses them, and they recover from their mental illness. Before start the prayer, people take a bath in the pond located in front of the temple. (Dhivya Dharsanam, 2008).

Mahandipur Balaji **Temple of Rajasthan:** The temple is located Dausa district of Rajasthan. This shrine has three worshippers deities: Balaji (Lord Hanuman), Pret Raj (The

King of spirits), and Bhairav. An artist never created the idol inside which is over more than 1000 years old and is believed to have self-appeared. As the legend goes, long ago, the image of Lord Balaji and that of Pret Raja (the king of spirits) appeared from the Aravali hills. People suffering from malignant spirits and black magic or spell got relief when they appealed for relief to Shri Bheruji Pret Raj Sankar, who holds his court and awards punishment to the malignant spirits, ghosts, goblins, ghouls, evil-eyed witches, etc. Many people claim to get relief here at the temple (Subudhi et al., 2020).

Other famous temples practicing temple healing are the Murugamalla temple, located in the Chikballapur District of Karnataka; Dattatreya Mandir, Gangapur is, located in Betul district Madhya Pradesh; and Devji Maharaj Mandir, Malajpur.

Mental Health Services in India

India is still in a dare state despite its effort to curb the issue of human resources shortage (Sinha & Kaur, 2011). The government has been making an effort to improve mental health services in the country. The National Mental Health Programme (NMHP) of 1982 and the DMHP of 1996 were meant to address the problem of human resources shortage. Despite the government's restless efforts, mental health services are still far from the target populations (Subudhi & Biswal, 2015).

Ministry of Health and Family Welfare (MHFW) (2007) says the country still faces a significant deficiency in health services the number of mental health experts and other facilities is still a challenge. The situation is much worse in rural where most people reside, and the problem rate is high. Inadequate mental health services, low literacy, socio-cultural barriers, religious beliefs, stigma, and

discrimination associated with mental illness hinder effective service delivery. World Health Organization (WHO, 2005) says that the people in rural areas cannot access the services of qualified doctors and other mental health professionals, where just 0.2 psychiatric, 0.05 psychiatrist nurses, and 0.03 psychologists are only available. In 2001 and 2005, the number of psychiatrists decreased (WHO, 2001), saying that India needed 140,000 psychiatrists. In contrast, we have about 3000 psychiatrists, and 75% of them work in urban areas where less than 28% of the population lives.

The role of EMH in dealing with mental illnesses

Studies have proved that cultural practices and religious beliefs have hindered people from seeking pharmaceutical assistance. Biswal et al. (2017) suggested empowering healthy minds to reduce the gap of human resources shortage. The EMH can be an ideal way to deal with the issue of mental illness. Empowering various support systems at the community level could increase awareness of mental health problems and stigma alleviation, especially in inaccessible areas. Through change agents like family, peer groups, relatives, and community members (Subudhi, 2021).

Mental health is a state of normal condition or situation where every human being is action efficiently towards themselves and their respective community; it is the absence of and freedom from mental illness and psychopathology (Herrman et al., 2005; Keyes, 2005). The difference between mental health and illness is just like health and illness, normal and abnormal, healthy and sick, sane and insane (Herrman et al., 2005; Keyes, 2005; Scheid and Brown, 2010). Mental health is something in a positive sense, and the absence of mental illness, but the lack of mental illness does not mean the presence of mental health (Keyes, 2005).

Mental health states the effective functioning of the mind; we can say that it is a state of subjective well-being. Mental illness occurs in the mind; it is a stage where a person may not be able to perform their social role appropriately (Subudhi, 2021)

Mental Illness

It is a very tough and critical job to attempt a study on human behavior, especially mental illness. Because the definition of mental illness has a variety of meanings in different cultures and times. The primary factor influencing the definition of mental illness is the majority of the people and/or by power institutions (Subudhi, 2021).

The Oxford dictionary of sociology defines "mental illness as a condition characterized by mental pathology: that is, disturbances, mental functioning, analogous to disturbances of bodily functioning" (Scott & Marshall, 2009). Thompson and Bland (1995) explained that mental illness is a chemical imbalance within our brain, a neurotic problem, and social dysfunction. Scott and Marshall (2009) mentioned mental illness is the judgment of the mind where deviance is one of the behavior.

Theories of Etiology of Mental Illness

The researcher has already explained the importance of culture on mental illness. The cultural sphere is highly dominant in the boundary of mental illness, including detection, description, management, and treatment. Most medical anthropologists have explained the causation of mental illness in the cross-cultural sphere.

Murdcok (1980) has classified the theories of the etiology of illness into two broad areas, i.e. natural causation and supernatural causation. Again he divided the supernatural causation of illness into mystical, animistic, and magical causation. Young (1976) classified the etiology of illness in medical perspectives into two broad areas (i) internalizing and (ii) externalizing. In internalizing, he accentuated physiological explanations, which include biophysical signs. In externalizing, he highlighted the links identifications between agencies/events with cause and effects.

The present study has followed the theories of illness given by Foster and Anderson (1978). He has mentioned that disease is a biological phenomenon and a cultural phenomenon. Human society has adopted new strategies to prevent and treat the disease. For that reason, man has developed vast knowledge, beliefs, techniques, and roles, norms … for a mutually reinforcing and supportive system. Hence, he divides the medical system into two major categories disease theory system and the health care system. The disease theory system deals with the beliefs about the nature of the health, causation of the illness, remedies, and curing techniques used by the doctors.

He identified two principal etiologies: personality and naturalistic, focusing on illness causality beliefs. Personality etiology focus on the "active, purposeful intervention of an agent, who may be human (a witch or a sorcerer), nonhuman (a ghost, an ancestor, an evil spirit), or supernatural (a deity or very powerful being). The sick person is a victim, the object of aggression or punishment, specifically accident or chance". There is an act of agent in all kinds of illnesses. Who is solely responsible for the illness?

In contrast with the personalistic theory, the naturalistic illness theory focused on impersonal, systemic terms. Illness is due to natural forces or conditions that may be cold, heat, winds, dampness, or imbalances of the humoral components of the body. It focuses on individuals' natural and social environment, health issues, and upsets in this balance that triggers illness

Summary

Chapter one discusses the importance of mental health research in the contemporary scenario and the influence of culture and religious places on managing a mental illness. The researchers have also highlighted mental health services in the country and their hindrances. The chapter also discusses the illness's etiological theories, including mental illness. The chapter has concluded with a discussion of different temple healing in India.

CHAPTER II

RESEARCH METHODOLOGY

Research methodology can be explained as a science of systematically analyzing how research is done (Kothari, 2004). A qualitative research method has been used to achieve the study's objectives. The researcher gathered comprehensive information from a few samples to capture participants' feelings, emotions, and perceptions of the research subject. The studied nature offers a complete description and analysis of a research subject and allows free and unlimited participant responses (Collins & Hussey, 2003). Furthermore, in this chapter, the researchers explain research objectives, research design, sampling, data collection and analysis, and ethical considerations.

Objectives of the Study

The study had the following objectives:

- To explore the explanatory models of mental illness among patients with mental illness and their family members attending the Chottanikkara Devi temple for healing.
- To explore the patients and their family member's experiences of temple healing at Chottanikkara Devi Temple.
- To document the healing process adopted by the Chottanikkara Devi temple.

Research Design

To achieve the objectives of the proposed study, the researcher has followed a qualitative methodology as qualitative research is a dynamic process that involves and links together problems, theories, and methods (Bryman &

Burgess, 1994). Flick (2018) says that the researcher picks a few constructs to provide clarity, insight, and understanding about issues or relationships in the social world in the qualitative study. The researcher opens up new theoretical insight, reveal distinctive aspects of people or social setting, or deepens understanding of the complex situation, events, or relationships. It focuses on the research topic rather than their representativeness, determining how people will be selected for the study. Research on mental health is crucial and different from other health-related investigations. Thus, while conducting mental health research, the researchers must be careful in choosing and applying the appropriate methodology (Subudhi & Biswal, 2020).

In the present study, the researcher has adopted medical anthropology. Because culture will show the healing process, medical anthropology will understand the healing (Samuel, 2015). Medical anthropology focuses on the cultural meaning of the illness. Foster and Anderson (1978) have mentioned that medical anthropology has helped the researcher comprehensively describe and interpret the bio-cultural interrelationship between human behavior and illness. It will help in-depth understanding between them.

Medical anthropology helps the researchers explore the labeling behavior of the mentally ill persons and their family member's beliefs in following traditional or biomedical healing practices and define the normal and abnormal behavior of a particular society. Psychiatrists and medical practitioners need to have an awareness and understanding of the emic perspective of the mental illness, which can help them better understand their patients, as it deals with normative beliefs, behavior, and accordingly provide better medication.

Each methodology has its strengths and limitations, and neither of them is sufficient to cover all the aspects of

mental health research. So both methods complement each other and help the researcher to carry out in-depth and intensive analysis in the mental health research (Subudhi & Biswal, 2020).

Medical anthropology fills three broad gaps in the epidemiological study, namely, (i) social, behavioral, and demographic characteristics of the patient who has a mental illness, (ii) geographical, ecological and social locales relationship with the mental illness, and (iii) onset of the mental illness and its risk factors (Dunn & Janes, 1986).

Sampling Design

Qualitative research usually concentrates on a small interview sample, either structured or unstructured, and focuses on the interview's cultural convention (Okely, 1994). The researcher has confined the sample size to 14 cases based on availability and time constrain. The sampling procedure has followed the purposive sampling method with inclusion and exclusion criteria.

Inclusion Criteria: People with mental illness and caregivers attend and stay at Chottanikkara temple for healing. ***Exclusion Criteria***: People with different kinds of diseases other than mental illness. Refuse to provide information.

Data Collection

Research Site: The researcher has got an aesthetic environment at Chottanikkara temple. Natural exospheres surround the temple. The famous Chottanikkara Devi temple is situated in Chottanikkara city near Ernakulam in Kerala. The chief Goddess of Chottanikkara temple is the Hindu mother, God Bhagavathi. The reason behind selecting the Chottanikkara temple as the research site is because the researcher wants to study the temple's healing practices among people with mental illness. The study was carried out in the year 2017.

***Reaching out for research*:** At the initial stages of the data collection, the researcher met the assistant commissioner of the Devasom Board of Chottanikkara temple and explained the study objectives, its nature, sample criteria, and its importance of the study. The researcher shared the interview guide, which helped the Kochin Devasom board understand the study's nature. After getting permission, the researcher started data collection.

Tools and Techniques of Data Collection

Qualitative research aids in understanding the phenomenon, which needs an in-depth understanding of the issue (Cresswell, 2013). The study used an in-depth interview method to learn about patients and their *emic* views of their illness. The researcher has used an interview schedule to get in-depth information from the respondents. The researcher followed different methods in this proposed research, including case histories, in-depth interviews, and observations, to collect information.

Explanatory models of illness highly accompany this schedule. The explanatory model interview schedule is based on previous researchers (Kleinman, 1980). As Kleinman (1978) defined, an explanatory model is the notion of an episode of sickness and its treatment employed by all those engaged in the clinical process. These models are linked to particular illness categories and reveal labels and cultural idioms for expressing their experience of illness. The interaction between the explanatory models of patients and practitioners is a central component of health care. The patient and practitioners explain how the practitioners understand and treat the sickness through the explanatory models. The explanatory models suggest how they make sense of given episodes of illness and how they choose and evaluate the particular treatment. The explanatory model explains sickness and treatment to guide choice among available therapies and therapists and cast personal and social meaning on the experience of sickness. Explanatory models must be distinguished from general beliefs belonging to the health ideology of the different health care sectors and exist independently and before a given episode of sickness.

Interview Process: In-depth interviews were conducted to collect the data from the respondents. This choice of data collection ensured that rich descriptive data emerged from the respondents and their expressions/ quotes of illness and experiences (Conrad, 1990).

Interview Setting: Interviews were conducted at Chottanikkara Devi temple among people with mental illness attending temple healing. In-depth interviews were conducted at the temple; an effort was made to ensure privacy in terms of spaces. Therefore, those respondents were free to express themselves. In all interviews, privacy was maintained.

Conducting Interviews: Before the interviews, the researcher explained the research purpose and the ethical issues that the researcher observed. In most situations, one case was interviewed several times depending on the information they shared and the willingness to spare more time for the interview.

Recording of Interview: The researcher used a tape recorder and field notes to record the interview process with prior permission from the respondents and their family members. In some cases, the respondents did not allow the researcher to use the tape recorder. In those cases, the researcher took hand notes, and later lengthy notes were written down immediately after the interview.

Transcription of the Interview: The interview was in Malayalam and Tamil by Somya SB (second author). Because she hails from Kerala State, the narratives were first written in Malayalam and then back translated to English.

Data Analysis

The study has adopted different coding patterns to analyze the collected information. Charmaz (1983) has mentioned that coding helps categorize and sort the data, and 'codes' will support summarizing and synthesizing the data. Different coding categories have been adopted for analyzing the open (initial coding) data, including axial coding. These codings are different from quantitative coding. Quantitative coding is based on preconceived, logically deduced code, while qualitative coding is a process of creating categories from the interpretation of data.

Operational Definitions

Healing and Healers

Healing is a process of relief from pain or restoring damage/deterioration and helps attain better functioning of the human organism. People use different healing practices for their illnesses, especially for mental illnesses. The person who provides healing is known as *Melshanthi* or high priest

Temple Healing

Temple healing is religious healing done in temples to cure people with (specifically in Hindu temples) mental illness. The prescribed healing varies according to the problem presented. Patients with '*paedi*' are given amulets, and patients with '*cheeta*' have prescribed chants and rituals at the temple. '*Guruthy* is for rid of evil spirits.

People with Mental Illness

People have mental health problems that affect their mental functioning and routine activities. It affects both the thought and feelings of an individual.

Ethical Considerations

Participation in this study was purely voluntary, and there was no compensation in terms of monetary or any other forms of benefit. The researcher clearly explained the objectives and purpose of the research to each respondent. Before collecting data, the researcher had obtained consent from the respondents and their family members. The researcher has kept all information related to respondents strictly confidential, and all information has been used only for research purposes.

Summary

The chapter discusses the methodological framework adopted for the study. The chapter starts with the objectives of the proposed research. The researcher has followed the qualitative methodology with the purposive sampling method to achieve the study's objectives. An overview of the research design has been presented. The chapter also described sampling, data collection, and data analysis procedures. At the end of the chapter, ethical considerations were discussed.

CHAPTER III

RESEARCH CONTEXT AND RESEARCHED

This chapter provides a brief insight into the proposed study's research site, respondents' demographic details, the onset of the illness, and the history of the disease among the respondents.

As stated in the previous chapters, the study was conducted at the Chottanikkara Devi temple. Chottanikkara Devi temple is in Chottanikkara, Kochi in Kerala. People believe that the Chottanikkara Goddess has the power to cure mental illness or the strength to strike the terror to evil forces. So, people suffering from mental illnesses commonly visit this temple believing that Chottanikkara Goddess will cure the disease of her devotees.

Eminence of the Chottanikara Devi Temple

The researcher has conducted a study at Chottanikkara temple about religious beliefs and healing practices. The below section gives a glimpse of the Chottanikkara temple.

Chottanikkara Devi Temple: Chottanikkara is a famous temple located in Chottanikkara, Kochi Kerala. Chottanikkara antiquity avails many historical and traditional divine stories. Its historical appeal attracts devotees from various places. The temple's area is believed to be infested by yakshas and raktharakshas. A devout worshipper of Kali named Kannappan lived in the area and would ritually sacrifice a cow to her every day. One day he got a calf, and his daughter was pleased and started petting the calf. Another day Kannapppan could not get a cow, and he wanted to kill the calf, but his daughter pleaded with her

father not to kill the calf. Kannappan was afraid to stop the offering.

At last, the daughter told her father to kill her first before he kills the helpless animals. It gave some sense into the senseless man after the incident; he never killed cows. Years after the death of his daughter, Goddess Bhagavathi appeared in his dream. She told him, 'you will find a cow in your cowshed, and that's me' next day, he found the cow and two stones (Krishnashila) in the cowshed. After the incident, everyone started praying; now, it has become the Chottanikkara temple (Pillai, 2008). Chottanikara Devi carries a stickle-headed sword and her right upper arm and *trisul* in her lower right arms, showing her determination and strength to strike terror into evil forces.

The temple is among the most visited and celebrated temples in India. The temple is dedicated to the Bhagavathy goddess, who has the power to cure mental illnesses and get rid of ghosts and evil spirits. Thousands of pilgrims and devotees visit and make offerings to redeem themselves from afflictions. In this temple, three feminine energies manifest Goddess mother Saraswati, who is worshiped in the morning; Goddess Lakshmi worshiped in the afternoon; mother Durga, worshiped in the evening. The temple's decorations also change three times a day. In the morning, the Goddess is worshipped in white clothes; in the afternoon, dark red and evening in blue clothes (Pillai, 2008). People suffering from mental illnesses commonly visit the temple, as Chottanikara Devi is believed to cure her devotees. The main *puja* of Chottanikkara Devi is *Athazha puja* and the *Athazhapuja* is main part of evening session.

Keezhkavu. Keezhkavu temple is found on the eastern part of the temple; it faces Chottanikkara Devi. A separate priest is appointed only for the Keezhkavu temple. We can see the central idol of Badrakali in the east of the pond. Mythologically the idol was installed by the Villamangalathu Swamiyar. He propagates the stories about the Devi. The main *puja* of Keezhkavu is Guruthi*puja*. After the *Athazha puja* of Chottanikkra temple, the chief priest makes *Valiyaguruthi puja* at Keezhkavu temple. Its starts at 8.45 pm every night. It is believed that if women attend *Guruthi puja* on Friday, they will be cured permanently of mental illness.

Figure 3.1: Chottanikkara Temple
(Photo by CR)

Respondents Profile

The sections discuss the respondents' socio-demographic details and their illness history. The data below indicates that all respondents came from rural areas, meaning the mental illness prevalence is higher in rural areas than in urban centers, which calls for special consideration. Furthermore, table 1 shows the level of education is another factor that seems to affect understanding and perception of mental illness and the type of healing people would seek. People with a medium and low level of education are the ones who still have strong beliefs in superstitions and believe evil spirits, which in the end determine the type of healing they will seek, causes mental issues.

Table 3.1: Demographic details of the respondents (Age, Sex Domicile, and Education)

Case	Age	Sex	Domicile	Qualification
Case 1	20	Female	Rural	Degree
Case 2	24	Female	Rural	Plus two
Case3	25	Female	Rural	Diploma
Case 4	38	Female	Rural	8th pass
Case 5	42	Female	Rural	6th pass
Case 6	38	Female	Rural	8th pass
Case 7	40	Male	Rural	10th pass
Case 8	45	Female	Rural	4th pass
Case 9	20	Female	Rural	9th pass
Case 10	48	Female	Urban	1st pass
Case 11	45	Female	Rural	1st pass
Case 12	27	Male	Rural	7th pass
Case 13	19	Female	Rural	8th pass
Case 14	21	Male	Rural	Degree

Table 3.2: Demographic details of the respondents (Marital Status, Work Status, Sibling, family status, and Family Income)

Case	Marital Status	Working Status	Siblings	Family status	Monthly Income (Rs)
Case 1	Single	NT	Two elder brothers	LCF	1000
Case 2	Married	NT	One younger brother	LCF	1500
Case 3	Single	NT	One younger sister and one younger sister	MCF	10000

Case 4	Married	NT	Two elder sisters	MCF	2000
Case 5	Married	NT	One elder brother	LCF	500
Case6	Married	NT	Two elder sisters and one younger brother	LCF	1500
Case 7	Married	Driver	One younger brother and one younger sister	LCF	1000
Case 8	Married	NT	Two elder sisters	LCF	1000
Case 9	Married	NT	One elder brother and two elder sisters	LCF	1000
Case 10	Married	Tailoring	one elder sister	MCF	10000
Case 11	Single	NT	two elder brothers	LCF	1000
Case12	Single	NT	One elder brother and one younger sister	LCF	1000
Case13	Single	NT	one younger case brother and one younger sister	LCF	1500
Case 14	Single	NT	one younger sister	MCF	5000

LCF: Lower class family; MCF: Middle-class family; NT: Not Working

The sample explains most of those who rely primarily on temple healing are people from low-income families. Data shows almost all of the respondents come from middle and low-income families. This suggests that inability to afford medication expenses leaves people with no option other than following the temple healing. Furthermore, the collected information shows that women of all ages, mostly in rural areas, are more likely to be subjected to mental issues.

Detailed Case Discussion

Case 1: Maheswari (*name changed*)

Demographic details: She is twenty years old and from Thirunnalveli, Tamil Nadu. She comes from a Hindu lower-class nuclear family consisting of a father, mother, and two elder brothers. She is studying Bachelor of Arts in English at Thirunnelveli Government College. Her father is 45 years old; he works in Gram panchayat as a sweeper, and her mother is 40 years old homemaker. Her elder brothers are 24 and 23 years old, respectively. They both stopped studying after the twelfth standard and now work as sales representatives in a textile shop. Her father is the breadwinner and head of the family.

Illness history: She developed a mental illness at the age of 18. She thought she was traumatized by the suicide event of her two colleagues, whom she thinks their evil spirits got her after their suicidal death. She believes that those evil spirits entered her body. After this incident, she started becoming aggressive and insomniac. She stopped taking food properly and started scolding Muslims, Christians, and Brahmins with slang. The changes happened mainly during the night times. One day her parents took her to a temple near her home. At that time, she behaved like a Muslim girl and started shouting and showing drowsiness. The evil spoke in the Tamil language and asked for notebooks, bags, dresses, etc. The process continued for five to ten minutes, and after that, she would be all right. Due to this problem, her parents met a folk healer. He told them about the evils that entered her body, and as those evil spirits wanted to study more, they used her body to gratify their needs. As per the suggestion by the folk healer, they did *poojas* and tried to fulfill the spirit's desires. But there were no changes in her behavior. After that, her parents took her to the hospital and did a complete body checkup and brain test. But the doctors couldn't diagnose any problem. One of her elder brother's friends told them about this Chottanikkara temple, and she came and stayed at the temple for five days. She ate ghee and followed all rules and regulations prescribed by the temple. After coming to the temple, she behaved abnormally by shouting at the deity and fainted. On the second day, one of the evils promised to leave her body. The priest took one hair from her head, twirled it in a nail, and hammered it in the *Pala* tree. The remaining spirits promised to leave her body the next day, and the whole ritual was repeated. However, after the *pooja,* she behaved normally. She believes more in temple healing than biomedicine. She told me that biomedicine couldn't cure her illness, and her family could not afford the expense of biomedicine. Other than some of her close relatives, no one knows about her condition. The family is trying to keep the issue a secret to avoid social stigma.

Case 2: Jayalakshmi (*name changed)*

Demographic details: She is 24 years old married lady staying in her parental home with her 4-year girl child. Her husband is separated from her and lives in his home. She was born and brought up in Venjaramood, Thiruvananthapuram. She is from a Hindu Ezhava lower-class nuclear family. Her father and mother separated nine years back, and her mother married another person who is now living with them. She has one younger brother who is 20 years old and working as a driver. She finished schooling at Government high school Venjarammod. After completing the twelfth, she joined in lab technician's course but discontinued after marriage.

Illness history; Got problems after her marriage. She was brilliant in academics, which made her friends and their parents jealous. She believes that they did black magic. That's why she got the problem. Due to this problem, she started suspicious of her mother and grandmother and behaved aggressively. Her grandmother went to meet an astrologer, and he told them about black magic. They did a lot of *poojas* as per the directions of the astrologer but couldn't cure her. After this, she consulted a psychiatrist and took medication for one month. The medicines were ineffective, and the financial crisis stopped her from continuing medication. Her relatives told her about the Chottanikkara temple during this time. She came to the temple and met the priest. He told her to do *Bajanam* (staying in the temple and attending *pooja*). She didn't have money to stay there, so she returned and came after two days. She visited the temple and stayed in a hotel room with her grandmother for 300 rupees per day. Her aggressive nature reduced gradually. She believes more in temple healing than biomedical treatment. She said that during the *Guruthi pooja* (one ritual performed by the temple), she became totally out of control and was unaware of what she did. No one in her family had a similar kind of illness. She doesn't share her disease with anyone. Her family members told her to visit a psychiatric hospital, but she was not willing, and moreover, she doesn't like her relatives for this reason.

Case 3: Geethu (*name changed)*

Demographic details: She is 25 years old. She is from a rural village of Ernakulam district, Kerala. She completed Diploma in Airline from Tamil Nadu. She is from a Hindu middle class nuclear family consisting of father, mother, one younger sister and brother. Her father is 55 years old. He studied till 10th standard and working abroad as a driver. Her mother is 45 years old, she too studied till 10th and she is a homemaker. Her younger sister completed nursing, she is 23 years old and she is working as a nurse and her younger brother is 19 years old studying Bachelor of science I visual communication in Ernakulum. Monthly income of the family is 10,000.

Illness history: she got problem at the age of 24. She used to faint during her study time but she and her parents thought that it resulted from learning and exam stress so they did not pay much attention to this. But her behavior changed completely after finishing her course. She stopped talking to others; she lost sleep and started talking and laughing to herself.

Due to this change in behavior, her parents took her to a mental hospital and admitted her there. But hospital made her more tired and half of her body got paralyzed after taking medicine. So her parents took her from the hospital. After that her father met a folk healer, he told that she doesn't have any mental disorder but affected by an evil spirit. Her mother told that before a year she removed three nails from a water tank. Folk healer told them that the evil spirit entered her body when she removed the nails.

A temple priest of nearby her home told them about Chottanikkra temple. The family came to the temple and met the main priest. He told them to attend *Bajanam* for four days, eat ghee and follow all the rules and regulations. When she came for the first time, she stayed with her mother in a nearby hotel room for 350 rupees per day. Her mother told that after reaching the temple, she changed a lot. Before coming there, she didn't not obey anyone and was more aggressive. After reaching there, she started obeying her mother and calm down a little. While planning to come to the temple, her mother was anxious about handling her, but everything went well. During the *Guruthi pooja* she doesn't do anything. No one had similar illnesses in her family. Her mother says that, her relatives and neighbors do not support her because they say it is a mental disorder so she needs psychiatric treatment. But she believes more in temples healing than modern medicine. She told that it is not mental disorder instead it is caused by evil spirit so, only God can cure her daughter.

Case 4: Baby (*name changed)*

Demographic details; She is 38 years old, married to Narayanan who is 48 years old who works as a farmer. She studied till 8th standard in a rural area in Palakkad. She is from a Hindu lower-class nuclear family consisting of husband and two children. She has a daughter and a son. Her daughter is studying in twelfth standard and son in 10th standard. They have been married for 10 years. The monthly income of the family is 2000.

Illness history; her problem started before six months with body pain, lack of initiative to do work. Some time she talked like small child. She took a full body checkup, CT scan and MRI scan but reports didn't show any problem. Then she met a healer. He told that it is an evil spirit and directed her to do some *pooja.* As per his direction they did the *poojas* but that was not useful. At the time her neighbours told her about *Chottanikkara* temple. She stayed in temple for five days. She behaved bizarre in the first day and became calm and started chanting mantras in the second day. She felt better and stopped talking like children. No one had similar kind of illness in her family. She stayed in *Devaswam* rooms and paid 300 rupees per day. Her husband and sister -in-law stayed with her. She believes in modern medicine but is not for mental illness. She prefers temple healing to biomedicine and her family cannot afford the cost for taking treatments. Her relatives and neighbours are supporting.

Case 5: Sumitha (*name changed)*

Demographic details: 42 year's old married woman from Trissur. She studied till sixth standard. She is from Hindu middle class nuclear family consisting of husband and two children. Her husband is Madhu. He is 45 years old, studied till 7th standard and he is working as driver. She has two children. Her son is 17 years old and completed twelfth. Her daughter is 13 years old and she is studying in 8th standard. Monthly income of the family is 500 rupees.

Illness history: her problem started before one month. She was attending National Rural Employment Guarantee Proramme (NREGP) and after the job she was walking alone through the road. Then she heard someone calling her name and turned back. That time she saw an evil and the evil entered her body. Her mother told that after the evil entered she started talking unnecessary things and laughing to herself. She started talking like another person. When her mother saw her, she understood that it is due to evil spirit so she took her to a temple nearby her home. At the temple, she behaved strangely and shouted in evil language. The temple priest told them about *Chottanikaraa* temple. After two days, she came to the temple and met the main priest. He told to do the *Bajanam* for 5 days and eat the ghee during the *bajanam*. She stayed in the temple for 3 days and followed all rules and regulation. She was aggressive during the *pooja* in Shiva temple and in *Guruthi pooja* session. It continued for 5 to 10 minutes after that she fainted and became all right. She stayed the *Devaswam* room by paying 300 rupees per day; her mother was staying with her. She says that after coming there she felt cured. She believes in biomedicine but she told bio medicine cannot cure her problem and temple healing is the best way of cure her illness. She did not go to any hospital before coming there. Because she knew that, it is a problem of possession. She told that temple healing can solve any kind of problem physical as well as mental but if we will take medication, it will harm our health. Moreover, she has no money for taking regular medication. In her family, no one has similar illness. Her mother told that, after coming there she started obeying so she had no problem managing her. She didn't share anything about her illness to her neighbours and friends in the fear of being teased by them. Her relatives are supportive.

Case 6: Suseela (*name changed)*

Demographic details; 38 year's old married woman. She is from Tamil Nadu. She studied till 8th standard and from a Hindu lower class nuclear family consisting of husband and three children. Her husband is Chella Pandi. He is 45 years old and working as a driver. Her elder son completed 10th standard and working as a mechanic second son is studying Polytechnic and the younger daughter is studying in twelfth standard. 1500 rupees is the monthly income of the family.

Illness history; she says that she got problem before one month. She saw an evil at nighttime in her home and she fell down. She was not normal after the vision. She met an astrologer and he told about *Chottanikkara* temple. She came and stayed in the temple for three days but could not attend the poojas as she is affected with stomach cancer. Before coming here, she did not go to any kind of psychiatric setting. She calls her problem as *payathakonam* in her local language. She is staying in hotel room near by the temple paying 200 rupees per day. Her sister-in-law is staying with her. She believes more in temple healing than modern medicine. She told that God can cure all kind of illness. She says that she saw so many people suffering from the problem of possession and cured their problem after coming here. She believes that she also will be. Her family has faced a lot of financial problems due to her diseases and they have no money to consult a psychiatrist. She says that neighbours and relatives are supporting her.

Case 7: Ullas (*name changed)*

Demographic details; He is 40 years married man. He is from Trissur. He studied till 10th standard. He comes from a Hindu lower class nuclear family consisting of his mother, wife and one daughter. His father passed away before 5 year ago. His mother is 78 years old and his wife is 34 years old. She completed 10th standard and she is a homemaker. His daughter she is 4 years old. He is an auto driver in a nearby town, the auto is taken for rent.1000 rupees is the monthly income of his family. He is the leader and bread winner of the family.

Illness history; He got problem 10 years back. He doesn't know how he got problem but he knows that evil entered his body. He suddenly collapsed, lost sleep and couldn't take food. Due to these problems, he met healer and as per suggestions, he attended poojas. But it turns out useless. He didn't meet any psychiatrist for his illness because he believed it is caused by evil spirits. His friend told him about *Chottanikkara* temple. He has attended *Bhajanam* three times and he stayed the temple for two weeks and another three weeks for attending all *poojas.* He feels cured but he says that once he leave the place another evil will enter his body and he can't be cured in this life time. He is staying in a hotel room paying 300 rupees per day. His mother staying with him. No one has similar kind illnesses in his family. His relatives and friends are teasing him for seeking indigenous treatment and temple healing. They are saying that he has some mental disorders and compelling to consult psychiatrist. No one believes that it is the possession problem. He told that if he took modern treatment it will affect his veins feel tired and he cannot do his work and he has no money for taking medicine properly.

Case 8: Radha (*name changed*)

Demographic details. She is 45 years old married woman. She is from Palakkad. She studied till 4th standard. She is from a Hindu lower class nuclear family consisting of husband and three children. Her husband is Balan, 49 years old, he is a coolly. Her elder daughter is Thulasi she studying degree third year. Second daughter is Thumitha she is studying degree first year and the younger son is Manoj, studying in 10th standard. 1000 rupees is the monthly income of her family.

Illness history; She got problem 15 years back. She fell down during her work and after that she started talking to herself. She started behaving aggressively to all. A folk healer she met told her that evil spirit is working in her body and it is the reason for all these problems. She started visiting temples and attending poojas but it was not useful. That time her husband's friend told them about *Chottanikkara* temple and she went to the temple and met the chief priest of the temple. He told to do *Bhajanam*. She has been staying in the temple for 14 days but there is no improvement. She didn't consult any psychiatrist, because she says that she has no mental problem. She believes temple healing than modern medicine. She is staying hotel room near by the temple paying 200 per day and her husband is staying with her. Her relative and neighbours are supporting her.

Case 9: Shivani (*name changed*)

Demographic details; She is 20 years old single girl. She is from Kozhikode. She is studying in 9th standard in Mukkam Government High School. She is from lower caste nuclear family consist of mother, one elder brother and two elder sisters. Her two elder sisters got married and her brother is 26 years old. He is a coolly. Her father passed away 10 years back and her mother is 60 years old and she is a coolly. 1000 is the monthly income of her family.

Illness history; she got problem at the age of 19. Her sister had problem of possession and she came *Chottanikkara* for *Bhajanam,* Shivani visited temple to see her sister but when she reached the temple she felt some sort of changes in her behaviour. They told her that she is possessed by the evil spirit of a 19 year old girl died in an accident. She speaks and behaves like that girl. That evil wants to live more and needs to fulfil her needs through this body. She has been staying in the temple for four days and she feels cured. She thinks that temple healing can cure all kind illness. She calls her illness in her local language *Bathakayari* (evil entered her body). She didn't take any kind of psychiatric consultation before coming here and her neighbours and relatives are supporting.

Case 10: Chithra (*name changed*)

Demographic details; She is a 48 year's old married woman. She studied till 1st standard. She is from Kollam. She is from a Hindu middle class nuclear family consisting of husband and one son. Her husband is Radhakrishnan, 52 years old, he studied till 7th standard and he is working in the construction field. Her son is Renjith, he is 29 years old he studied till 10th standard and working as a driver now. Her husband and son are working in Bangalooru so she is also settled there. Her husband is the leader and bread winner of the family.

Illness history; she got problem 3 years back. She started talking and laughing to herself and started picking up fights with neighbors. Her neighbors told her husband that she is behaving like this due to evil spirit and advised him to take her to any healers or temple. So, her husband took her to a healer. The healer informed them about the evil spirit and told them to attend *poojas* but no result was visible. After one year of temple healing she consulted a doctor from National Institute of Mental Health and Neuroscience (NIMHANS) and the doctor told her that she has some psychiatric problems. As per the doctor's advice, she took medication for one and half year. But she didn't feel any cure and she get more tired due to heavy medication. She believed that what she suffers is the problem caused by evil spirits so she stopped her medication. That time her relatives told her about *Chottanikkara* temple. She came and stayed in temple for four days doing *Bhajanam,* after reaching the temple she felt some changes in her behaviour. She could sleep properly and it reduced her aggressive behaviour. She believes more in temple healing. She told that bio medicine can't cure all problems especially that caused by the evil spirits. No one in her family has similar illness. When she gets problem she become more aggressive and tries to attack any one. She is staying *Devaswam* rooms and paying 350 rupees per day. Her son and sister in law are staying with her. Her neighbours and relatives are supporting her

Case 11: Valsala (*name changed)*

Demographic details; She is 45 years old married woman coming from Kottayam. She studied till 4th standard and she is working as tailor. She belongs to a Hindu lower class nuclear family. She has two daughters. Her elder daughter is Vijayalakshmi. She is 22 years old and studying TTC. Her younger daughter is 17 years old and she is studying in twelfth standard. She is the leader and the bread winner of the family.

Illness history; she got problem 15 years ago due to black magic of her mother. She came to know from a nearby temple that someone is doing black magic on her. She behaved abnormally, shouted and danced in the temple. Then she met an astrologer who told her that her mother did black magic on her because she wanted her property. She knew about *Chottanikkara* temple because it is a famous temple in Kerala.10 years back she stayed in temple for 10 to 15 days ad left when she felt cured. She says that when she is in the temple she feels cured but when she go back home, the black magic starts working again. She didn't consult any kind of psychiatrist so far because she thinks it is the work of evil spirits. She believes more in temple healing practice than modern medicine. She said that she separated from her husband10 years back due to black magic of her mother. Now she came to the temple just for worshipping but after reaching here she came to know that evil is still working in her body. When she gets problem, she become unconscious and starts shouting and feel drowsy. She stays in temple premises. She cannot afford a hotel room due to financial problem. She didn't eat ghee (priest give ghee for curing the illness) She is staying alone in temple. Her family members and neighbours told her that she is a mental patient and that they will never accept it as a problem caused by evil spirits. She called her problem *Kudothram* (black magic) in local language.

Case 12: Subhramanyan (*name changed)*

Demographic details; He is 27 years old and he is from Malapuram. He studied till 7th standard. He is from Hindu lower-class nuclear family consisting of father mother and one elder brother and one younger sister. His father is Kumaran he studied till 1st class and he is a coolly. His mother is Vijaya she studied till 4th standard and she is a home maker. His elder brother is Vijeesh. He finished 10th standard and doing construction work. His younger sister is Vijitha she studied till 10th standard and got married. His father is the leader and bread winner of the family.1000 is the monthly income of the family.

Illness history; He got problem at the age of 12 because he saw a supernatural power in the night. In his childhood, he was staying with his grandfather and saw something strange one night which inflicted fear in him. His parents took him to healers nearby his home and do lots of *pooja* for curing his illness and visit many temples but nothing changed. That time his relatives told them to consult a psychiatrist. He took medication for 5 years with no improvement. When he got problem he shows fearful face and sit alone. Presence of other people makes him fearful and he tries to run away from home. His relatives told about *Chottanikkara* temple. He stayed in temple for 6 days, first time visiting the temple he didn't feel cured because he never followed the rules of the temple and didn't eat ghee. But after reaching here his personal hygiene improved and wandering tendency decreased. He is staying in Devasom room with his mother and elder brother and paying 275 per day. He believes more in temple healing and religious healing because taking bio medicine will cause tiredness and reduce the immune capacity. Bio medicine is expensive also. His relatives and neighbours do not support him, and is avoided from functions and social gatherings.

Case 13: Jeeva (*name changed)*

Demographic details; She is 19 years old coming from Erode, Tamil Nadu. She studied till 8th standard. She is from a Hindu lower class nuclear family consisting of father mother and a younger brother and sister. Her father is Sundran, 37 years old and he is a coolly. Her mother is Lakshmi, 35 years old and she is a home maker. Her younger sister sobhana, is 18 years old and studied till twelfth standard. Her younger brother is Chandru. He studied till 7th standard stopped going school. 2000 is the monthly income of the family. His father is the leader and bread winner of the family.

Illness history; she got problem at the age 13. She behaved like a 5-year-old child. So her parents took her to the hospital and the doctor told them that her brain function is delayed. They was treated for a year with no improvement. She doesn't know how to talk and behave to others. It was then her family members told that it is an evil spirit and instructed to take her to folk healers. They went to healers and did pooja. But nothing changed. That time she came to know about *Chottanikkara* through her relatives came there and stayed there for 10 days. There were slight differences in her behaviour even after coming to temple. But she believes in temple healing because she heard a lot of stories and saw many devotees cured from their illnesses from there. She believes in religious healing than modern medicine. Bio medicine is more expensive and she has no money for bio medicine. She is staying in temple premises due to lack of money. Her mother is staying with her. Relatives and neighbours are blaming her due to her problem.

Case 14: Akhil (*name changed*)

Demographic details; He is 21 years old from Thrissur. He completed graduation and joined for IAS coaching.. He is from a Hindu middle class nuclear family consisting of father, mother and one younger sister. His father is Chandran who is 52 years old, working as a driver. His mother Sheeja who is 49 years old and a homemaker. Her younger sister Akhila is 19 years old and she is pursuing her degree. 400 is the monthly income of the family.

Illness history; He got the problem at the age of 21st due to failing in IAS exam. After exam he showed no interest in talking to others especially his parents. He didn't sleep

well and eat properly. He started talking irrelevant things, his relatives and others told them that it is because of possession problem. His parents took him to folk healers and attended *poojas* but there was no change in his behaviour. His father's friend told them about *Chottanikkara* temple. Before coming here, he didn't take any psychiatric consultation from hospital because his parents didn't accept his problem as psychiatric. He didn't feel any change when he came there for first time. He stayed at the temple for four days. They believe more in temple healing than bio medicine for all types of diseases. They didn't share anything about illness to anyone because they feared it may spoil his future life. He stayed in hotel room with father mother, grandmother and uncle and paid 300 rupees per day.

Summary

The chapter highlights the respondent's religious belief system towards mental illness and their help-seeking pattern of mental illness. This contextual background would facilitate the reader to understand the respondent's belief system towards mental illness and how the cultural beliefs relate to healing practices. The respondents and their views/experiences have been continuously referred in this chapter. Furthermore, the above-shared stories portrayed detailed information and a strong belief that the patients, families, friends, or neighbors carry on temple healing. The data also shows that most of those seeking temple healing come from lower- and middle-income families.

CHAPTER IV

PERCEIVED BELIEFS AND MENTAL ILLNESS

History of mental illness says that people's beliefs in supernatural powers cause mental illness. The condition was viewed as the result of malicious influence exercised by supernatural forces or another human being. And some temples have become a treatment point for various illnesses, especially mental illness, and the temple has been used as a place of healing for incubation or temple sleep. Dube (1970), many misconceptions, superstitions, and ignorance exist, mental goddess or of a curse exaggerated beliefs in mystic influences, and excessive faith in the power of saints, priests, and medicaments (Subudhi & Biswal, 2021).). Banerjee and Roy (1998) studied severe mental disorders at temples and other religious places in India. Beliefs in magico-religious causes of physical and psychological disease are deeply ingrained in the minds of the Indian masses, even in populations with higher literacy. Every society has its own culture, which regulates individuals' perception and treatment procedures of mental illness. Srivastava (2002) has mentioned three different theories of causation of mental illness; supernatural theory, shock theory, and biomedical theory. In the supernatural view, he said the possession of a maleficent evil/soul causes a change in a person's psychology and makes the person mentally ill. Most of the people believe in supernatural causation, and they approach some faith healers to remove the evil spirit from their bodies. In shock theory, he mentioned it makes a sudden change in the environment, and the person can't cope with these situations; its leads to mental illness.

The chapter covers the *emic* perspective of mental illness. It covers the respondents' opinion, and experience about the etiology of mental illness, the meaning of local nomenclatures of mental illness, during spirit catches the body, and priest opinion about mental illness.

Patient and family members' opinions about mental illness

Most respondents believed that a mental illness is an illness of the mind. The doctors' use of medicine and consultation to fight the illness will continue till the end of life. The respondents believed that they are facing the problem due to evil spirits, which is different from mental illness. The evil spirit enters their body in various situations in life. Maybe it's from the workplace, when they walk alone in the afternoon, go around the temple, and do black magic, etc. The respondents believed that the evil spirit entered their bodies to fulfill their needs with help.

The majority of the family members of the respondents believed that mental illness is different from other types of health-related illness, not a curable disease till the end of life. But possessing an evil spirit is different, and it can be cured with the help of God.

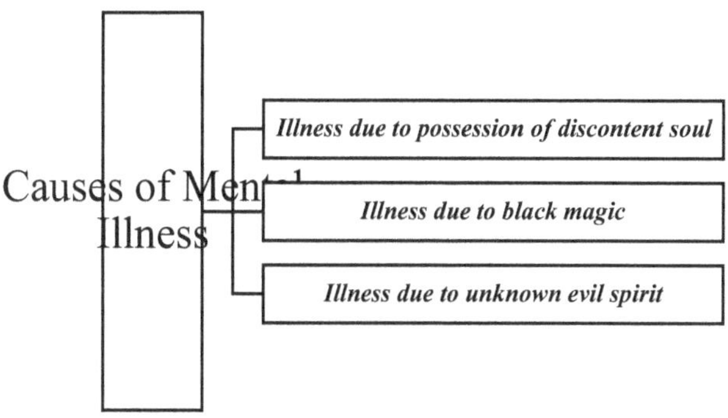

Figure 4. 1 Causation of mental illness shared by the respondents

Illness due to possession of the discontent soul

One of the respondents, Maheswari, said she suffers from an illness due to discontent spirit. She said three students committed suicide in their college without gratifying their wishes. These three evil spirits entered my body to fulfill their desires with the help of my body. Three evils needed to study more, so they asked for notebooks, school bags, uniforms, etc. She said the evils can not be removed if they do not gratify their wishes.

Illness due to black magic

Geethu said that she was suffering from black magic. She said her neighbors are jealous of her because her family is more financially stable than her neighbors. One day, she went on top of her house and saw three nails hammered on the water tank. She removed the nails from the water tank. The evil spirit entered her body when she pulled the nails from there. She said that her neighbors saw a black witch hammer the nails on the water tank at the top of her home to interrupt their financial growth.

The researched Jayalakshmi said that she got the problem due to black magic. She is brilliant in her studies and scored good marks. So, her friends and their parents were jealous of her. So, with the help of a black magician, they did black magic on her.

In another researched Valasala said that she is suffering due to black magic. She said that her mother did black magic on her for her property.

Illness due to an unknown evil spirit

The researched Baby said that, she got a problem due to unknown evil spirit. She said, she behaved like child and crying for unnecessary things. So, her husband went to meet an astrologer with the guidance from neighbors. After that, she came to know that one possession of evil spirit entered in her body. She said, she doesn't know how the evil spirit enter her body

The researched Suseela said that she got the problem due to the unknown evil spirit possession. She said that she went to the back side of her home one day to take warm cloth Suddenly, she heard strange sound behind her. And she torn back. She saw the evil spirit stand there and she fainted. After the incident she showed some behavioral changes. She said the behavioral changes happened because the evil spirit enters her body.

Jeeva said she got a problem due to possession of evils, she is 19 years old but behaves like 10 years' girl. So, the neighbors told her patents to meet folk healer. After that, she realized the problem is due to possession of evil. But she doesn't know how the evil spirit enters her body.

Subramanyan told that he got illness due to possession of evils. In his childhood he saw evil spirit during night time and he scared. He said that time the evil spirit enters his body. His parents took him to folk healer after that he came to know the evil spirit work in his body.

Chithra said that she started talking unnecessary things, laughing, and fighting with neighbors. She said she can't sleep and eat properly. Due to her behavioral changes her husband went to meet a folk healer, then only she knows that the problem is due to possession of unknown evil spirit.

Radha told that, one day she fainted at work place after that she seem to behave unusual like self-talking, laughing, and aggressive behavior etc. she said she can't sleep properly. So, she went to meet an astrologer he guided her that its problem due to evil spirit.

Ullas told he got illness due to possessed by unknown evil spirit. One day suddenly he lost his sleep and behaves more aggressive. So, he met one astrologer and came to know it's due to evil spirit.

Akhil told that he was failed IAS exam after that he didn't talk to other especially his parents, lost her sleep, and start to talk irrelevant things. Due to his problem parents took him folk healer. The folk healer guided him that he is suffering the problem due to possession of evil spirit.

Sumitha told that the evil spirit enters her body when she was return from her work place. One day she came back alone from her work place. She heard some strange sound behind her and she turned back and evil spirit entered her body. After this incident she had some behavioral changes like laughing to herself, talking unnecessary things, such things. She said her mother understood that the evil spirit enter her body.

Local Nomenclature of Mental Illness

In Chottanikkara temple there are different kinds of people coming for curing their mental illness process. The people are using different nomenclature for their mental illness: *Peipudichirk, Kudothram, PayathaGunam, Badha. Pei pudichirk* is a Tamil word used to denote possession of evil spirit. *Kudothram* is a Malayalam word, which mean black magic. *payathagunam*is a Tamil term is meaning that fearful or scaring, *Badhakayari* is a Malayalam term is meaning that evil enter the body.

During spirit catches the body/patient's condition during evil possession

The findings show that almost all participants believed that evil spirits and possessions were mental illness's main etiology. Maheswari's brother said three evils possess his sister's body, which entered her body on her way from college. When the evil got into her body, she behaved like three characters. Commonly the problem arises during the night times that time she lies like a piece of wood and she clutches her teeth together. Sometimes her face also changed like evils.

Sumitha's mother explained that she got a problem from her workplace. One afternoon she was walking alone on the road going to eat lunch, that time she heard a strange sound so she turned back and saw the evil which entered her body. If she didn't look back, she would have been saved. If the evils come to her body, she will behave aggressively and shout to others.

Son in law said that when the problem rises she will start to speak like a child and crying and asking for Chocolate from him.

Jayalakshmi's Grandmother said that she starts to behave aggressively when the problem arises.

Geethu told that when the evil souls enters her body she starts to talk to self, self-laughing, and act very aggressively.

Akhil's mother said he would start to speak irrelevant and cry when the evil spirits possessed his body.

Most of the respondents behaved very aggressively, shouting to the family members when spirit/soul enters their body.

Priest opinion about mental illness

Chottanikkara Devi temple chief priest said that many people come to the temple from different places to cure their illnesses. He said that mental illness affects the mind and is due to external fear, exam fear, possession of evil, and marriage between close relationships. Lots of devotees visit the temple daily to heal their illness. The people speak like evils in front of Devi and behave like evils. After three or four days, they feel better with the help of Devi. Chottanikkara Devi has the power to cure their illness. He believes that if the people wear chanted Chakras from the Chottanikkara temple, possession of evil will not attack.

Summary

People with mental illness tend to experience periodic fears and believe that the forces are more vital beyond the human ability to fight them. The study found out that being in the temple give them a sense of peace and security which help calm their mind. People believe the cause of mental illness is due to evil spirits, black magic, and external fears. Here, the research found that the astrologer confirms the confirmation about the supernatural etiology of illness. Most of them find temple priests, astrologers, or folk healers to cure their ailments. These sources strengthen the respondent's belief systems.

CHAPTER V

HEALING PRACTICES AT CHOTTANIKKARA DEVI TEMPLE

Temple healing is a therapeutic intervention that involves both the conscious and unconscious mind and is associated with subjective meaning. It focuses on the somatic mode of treatment. It is a placebo effect, and there is no argumentative theory to heal the illness (Samuel, 2015). People believe that supernatural causes result from mental illness, and most people use traditional healing practices to address mental illness. Trivedi and Sethi (1980) and Thara et al. (1998) say that up to 70% to 80% of the population of mentally ill belong to rural areas and first visit religious places and consult with the indigenous practitioners for their treatment. Even eight out of ten patients with mentally ill are seen at religious healing centers. Raghuram et al. (2002) have mentioned that both the elite literature of traditional culture and the so-called higher civilization of today agree on the same fact.

People with mental illnesses associated with evil spirits are more inclined to spiritual and traditional healing. Their belief and perception of the source of illness is a greater determinant of type of healing they will seek. But first, they consult only the traditional healers only. Most people believe that their faith played a significant role in their recovery. The meaning these patients put on their spirituality is that it helped them to cope with difficult times, gave them a sense of usefulness, allowed them to feel a part of (as in fellowship), gave them peace and comfort, and provided them with a sense of purpose.

This chapter covers the following components: (i) healing procedures od mental illness at Chottanikkara Devi temple; (ii) opinion and experience of the patient about the healing practices at Chottanikkara temple

Healing Practices at Chottanikkara Temple

The Chottanikkara Temple practices the following practices for people with mental illness to heal their mental illness. All the patients are expected to attain all the *pooja* and follow all the regulations practiced by the temple. Those who decided to do or sit for Bhajana should arrive at the temple on the previous day and after having *Nirmallya Dharshanam*. The following day should start the *Bhajana* after the *Nirmalla*[1]*Dharshan*. Both the *Devis Melkavu* and *Keezhkavu* should do *pradakshinakshinam*[2] in the temple.

In simple terms, walk around the *nalambalabalam*[3] chanting the Nama of Devi (*Namajapam*). After that, prostrate before Lord Shiva during *Dhara*[4]and prostrate before the Melkavu Devi during the *Ethritha Pooja*. Then do Pradishanam again doing *seevenly*[5]. Keep it safe after that prayer, bow during Guruthi in Keeahkavu, and receive Guruthi Prasadam. Then pray and bow before Devi during Pantheeradi[6] Pooja in Melkavu. And receive and consume *Bhajana ghee*. After *GuruthiPrasatham,* the mental illness patients are allowed to take their breakfast food. After breakfast, do *Pradakashinas* in the temple chanting the *Namas* of Devi. Pray before the *Sreekovil* of lord Shiva during *Dhara,* before Devi during the noon *Pooja* at Melkavu, and noon *Seevaly*. Receive the *Nivedhya* rice and take it for lunch.

---

[1]First *pooja* in the morning is called nirmalyam and attend morning *pooja is called nirmalya darahanam*

[2] Circumambulation

[3] Surrounding of the temple

[4] Sprinkling the holly water to the devotees

[5]Ritual of the temple

[6]Decoration of the temple by flower

Sleeping during the daytime should undoubtedly be avoided. Prayer and boo before the deities in Melkavu and Keezhkavu when the temple opens in the evening and do Pradakhshinam as before. During Deeparadhana, Athazha pooja, and Seeveli in Melkavu, Pray has *Guruthipoojaand Darshan* in Keezhakavu. Receive *GuruthiPrsadam* and eat the same; they have food at night. Avoid food from outside. Pure food is usually prepared with a minimum of salt, tamarind, and chilies for patients. The best is to eat fruits and drink milk. Those who are doing *Bhajana* should not go out of the temple premises. Special attention must be paid to see to those who do *Bhajana.*

Experience of Temple Healing at Chottanikkara

Table 5.1: Source of Getting Information about the Temple

Source of information	Number of patients
Friends (brother's close friends, husband friends, father friends)	4
Family member(husband-wife, grandmother, brother in law)	3
A priest nearby the home	3
Neighbors	2
Already knows about the temple	2

Table 5.1 shows that majority of the patient got information from close friends, family members, and the priest from the temple nearby home. Two of the respondents got information from neighbors, and the rest of them already knew about the temple. But close friends are the light source of getting information about the temple. These close friends include the brothers', father's, and husband's friends.

Table 5.2: Number of days completed at the temple for healing at the time of data collection

Name of the Patients	**No of days staying**
Maheswari, Baby	5
Suseela, Geethu	6
Jayalakshmi, Akhil	3
Sumitha, Subhramayan	7
Jeeva	12
Valasala, Radha, Ullas	17
Chithra, Sivani	4

Patients are being stayed there for the given days when the researcher met them.

Respondents' Past Experience at Chottanikkara Temple

Only two patients (Ullas and Vasala) informed that they had previous experience at *Chottanikkara* temple. Ullas came here ten years back. During that time, he had been here for five days. After that, he felt better and returned to his home. He informed us that this illness is not curable during this interaction with him. At the time of healing, one evil leaves his body after attending the healing practices. When he goes back home, another evil will get into his body. The researcher felt that the condition is the relapse of the illness. Valsala came to the temple five years back due to black magic and cured her problem. Now again, she got a problem due to black magic. The rest of the patients (12) was on their first visit to the temple.

Daily Practices

The temple prescribes all the practices for all the patients. The daily routines start in the early morning at 4. 00 am and continue until 9.30 pm. All patients should attend all *pooja* prescribed by the Chottanikkra temple. Following are the daily practices followed by the Chottanikkara temple. The temple will open at 4.00 am and attend the Nirmalya darshan. After the Nirmalyadarshan, the respondents should do so *Pradakshinam* in the temple in both the Devis in Melkavu and Keezhkavu. In simple terms walk around the *Nalambalam* chanting the nama of Devi (Namajapam). After that, prostrate before during the *Ethirtha pooja*. Then do *pradakshinam* again during *Seeveli*. After that, pray and how during Guruthi *prasadam* and keep it safe. Then pray and bow before Devi during *Pantheereadi pooja* in Melkavu and receive and consume *Bhajana ghee*. After that *Guruthi prasadam* will be taken by the patients. Then only take breakfast. After breakfast, do *Pradakhshinas* in in the temple, chanting the Namas (names) of the Devi. Pray before the *Sreekovil* of lord Shiva during *Dhara*, before Devi during the noon *pooja* at Melkavu, and at noon *Seeveli*. After *Seeveli* receive *Nivedya* rice and take it for lunch. After that, get some time for rest, but sleeping during the daytime is not permissible. Keezhkavu.

Healing practices during the menstruation Time

During their menstruation days, the female devotees and those attending them must leave the temple based on the Hindu religion rules and return to the temple premises only after seven days.

In the research, eleven of the respondents were female. Two (Shivani, Geethu) respondents told that during menstruation, they will go home with the help of chanted thread and come back after menstruation. Nine respondents said they planned when the menstrual cycle would happen before the coming temple and came to *Bajanam* accordingly.

Opinion about the Guruthi Pooja

Guruthi pooja is one of the main rituals performed by the Chottanikkara temple. It starts at 8.30 pm and goes up to 9.30 pm. The main priest said that; if the patient attends Guruthi pooja every Friday, it will help permanent cure from mental illness. Nine respondents said that they become unconscious during the *Giruthi* pooja session and are unaware of what they are doing. Maheswari said that, during the Guruthi pooja, her evil starts to talk; that time, she will dance, shout and scold to God, etc. After *Guruthi pooja* she feels better. And she told during the *Guruthi pooja,* the Keezhkavil Amma tried to remove evil from her body. Most respondents said they are unconscious and don't know what they are doing during the Gurutthi pooja session but feel better after the *Guruthi pooja*. Four respondents said they didn't feel any change in her behavior during the *Guruthi pooja.*

Researcher Experience with Guruthi Pooja

During the study period, the researcher got an opportunity to be a part of the *Guruthi pooja*. The Chottanikkara temple performs the ritual and a special *pooja* in Keezhkavu temple. It starts every day night at 8.30 pm and continues till 9.30 pm. Believe that *Athazha pooja* is for Chottanikkara Devi and *Valiya Guruthi pooja* for Keezhkavu Bhagavathi. *Athazha pooja* is the main part of the evening session. After the *Athazha pooja* the chief priest makes *Valiya Guruthi* at Keezhkavu temple. Many people come from different places to attend the *Guruthi Pooja*. The people believed that if the person with mentally ill will attain the *Guruthi Pooja* on Friday, it would give them relief from mental illness.

The researcher got a great experience in the *Guruthi* pooja session. During *the Guruthi pooja,* people with mental illness behave like evils. They were shouting, dancing, and walking continuously like evils. They speak like evils, and some patients act like God/Goddesses. The *Keeezhkavu* makes the place resound with *Bhakti* filled *Namajapams* (chanting mantras) accompanied by instrumental music (*Chendamelam*). The music tone was exceptional; it can easily influence people's minds and put the devotees on a high spiritual level. They beat the drum flows from high to middle and then lower pitch. Normal people also feel the change and disturb their minds due to the music frequency. It was a new experience for the researcher.

Sacred Trees

One Banyan tree and three Palai (*Alstonia scholaris*) trees are there in the premises of Chottanikkara temple. It carries hundreds of steel nails, baby dolls, and different red and black colored clothes tied in the tree. It shows that the devotees were ready to surround after the *pooja*. We can see the first Palai on the right side of the Sastha temple, the other two situated on the right-left side of Keezhkavu, and one nearest to Keezhkavu temple. The *Palai* trees carry hundreds of nails, thread, bungles, silk, etc. These declare that the devotees concerned have been exorcised here.

Figure 5.1: The Banyan Tree
(P.C. by CR)

Effects of the Temple Healing

The temple's history shows that many people came from different parts of India to cure their illnesses, and many people fixed their illnesses. Patients highly believe in the temple healing practices. They think that God will heal their illness. In this research, ten respondents feel the change after coming here. The respondents said they were very aggressive and uncontrolled before coming here. They had severe health complications like body pain, sleeplessness, and low appetite. After reaching the temple, they observe and felling some changes in their behavior.

During the interaction with Maheswari, she said that after attending the healing practice of the temple, she feels better and is being cured. She told Before coming to the temple; three evils were working in her body. On the second day at the temple, one evil left her body, and the priest took one hair from her, tied hair in the nail, and nailed it to the Palai trees. Two other evils were also left from her body on the third day. Through the same process, remove the evils from her body. Now she feels better.

Four of the respondents didn't feel recovery after coming here. They said they stayed in the temple from seventeen to eighteen days but did not feel any change in their illness. However, they have a strong belief in the Goddess of the temple. Geethu said that she stayed at the temple for six days and felt little changes in her behavior, such as reducing her aggressiveness, obeying her mother, sleeping well, etc. Suseela, Jeeva, Ullas, and Radha do not feel any changes, and Suseela said she doesn't feel cured because she didn't attend all pooja in the temple due to her health problem. Sumitha, Valasala, and Sivani feel cured after reaching the temple.

Opinion about Temple Healing

All of the respondents have more faith on the Chottanikkara temple. The respondents had heard lots of stories about Chottanikkara Amma. Most respondents said Chottanikkara amma has excellent power to cure all devotees' illnesses. Biomedicine is not helpful in mental illness, and temple healing has the supreme power to remove the possession and evil spirits. Lots of people have the experience of curing their problem of evil spirits.

Life of the Patients during Temple Healing

The respondents were staying with family members and relatives. One of the respondents stayed alone in the temple because she came for one day, but she realized that she was possessed by black magic after reaching here. Seven respondents stayed in nearby hotels, and they were paying □ 200 to □ 600 per day. Those respondents remained in the Devasom rooms; they were paying □ 350 per day. Four respondents were staying at the temple premises due to financial difficulties. They said that they are getting support from their relatives and neighbors. Five respondents said they had not shared their illness with anyone due to social stigma.

Priest Opinion about Healing Practices

The Chottanikkara Devi temple provides healing practices to cure mental illness. They should follow and attend all *pooja* of the temple and obey the temple's rules. The priest said there is no assurance of complete cure, but the feasibility of relapses is inevitably there. The priest said that if the patient attended all *pooja* of Chottanikkara temple with the belief that it would cure the mental illness. He said that if the patient attends *Guruthi pooja* at Keezhkavu every Friday, it will help permanent cure from mental illness, and lots of people leave the place with getting cured. The patient should eat *Bhajana ghee and* then only take breakfast. The devotees should follow all rules and regulations provided by the temple.

Opinions about Allopathic treatment

The respondents viewed that allopathic is only applicable to people's physiological health, not to mental health. People have blind beliefs that mental illness is caused by the evil spirit, black magic, and external fear. Hence, Allopathic is not applicable, and it has side effects also. Ullas said that continuous medicine causes health problems, and he can't afford the allopathic medicine cost.

Most of the respondents have a financial problems in taking Allopathic medicine. Geethu and Chithra said that they were taking Allopathic medicines before coming here but couldn't get any changes in their illness. But the patient felt tired due to allopathic medicines. Geethu said that one side of her body was paralyzed due to taking drugs. She said it is not a health problem. The rest of the respondents have no experience in Allopathic medicine. They don't use the medication because they don't believe in Allopathic

treatment. Study by Subudhi et al. (2020) on willingness on hospital stay among the patients shows that, the patients and their family members are expressing their interest not stay in the hospital because of the loss of identity, disruption in the family routine activities, unfriendly indoor patients ward.

Table 5.3: Preference for healing at the onset of illness

Healing Procedure			
Temple	Astrologer	Folk healers	Psychiatrist
3	4	6	1

The respondents considered the illness due to evil spirit and black magic, so they preferred to consult folk healers and indigenous medicine to cure the onset of illness. The above table 5.3 shows that six of the respondents consulted folk healers for their onset of disease and four respondents consulted an astrologer for their illness at the beginning. Three of the respondents first went to the temple to cure their onset of illness. And only one respondent went to meet a psychiatrist for her onset of disease. This table shows that most people believe in traditional practices for curing their illnesses at the time of onset.

Summary

This chapter discusses the healing practices followed by the Chottanikkara temple and the patient's experiences and opinions about temple healing. In Chottanikkara, the numbers of people visit to cure their ailments. The study said that family members and friends influence people to seek temple healing practices for mental illness. In this research, the respondents said they got information from close friends, family members, and priests from the temple nearby home. The patients will stay and follow all rules and regulations the temple prescribes to cure their mental illness. The respondents said they would remain in the temple until they fixed their disease in this research.

Most respondents believed that temple healing practices to cure their illnesses and make them feel better after reaching the temple. The temple's history tells that the number of mentally ill people came to the temple and cured their illnesses. Many people who are trebled by emotional distress or severe mental illness prefer to go to religious centers to heal their problems. Most people believe in religious institutions and then consult these institutions for healing.

CHAPTER VI

EPILOGUE

People believed that mental illness was due to supernatural power, magical spirit, or possession by evil spirits in the ancient period. The 21st century has seen many changes in all walks of human life. The standard of life has increased to a great extent. The changes in education policies created a leap in the number of educated people. Economics, trade, and technology are the palm of change and development. Still, our attitude towards religious practices and culture has not changed very much. The high quality of education we receive from the educational institutes fails to keep us away from our adherence and submission to religious practices. Even now, in healing mental and physical ailments, people seek assistance from these old age traditions, and most prefer traditional healing practices to address mental illness.

In India, many people visit religious centers to cure their mental illnesses. Many temples are famous for healing mental illness. Chottanikkara Temple is one of thhem. Many people visit the temple to cure their diseases daily, and legends of the temple revealed that many people had cured their illnesses at Chottanikkara temple. The people attend all *pooja* at Chottanikkara and usually take Ghee from the temple. The person with mental illness should attend *Guruthi Pooja* as it is believed that if the person attends *Guruthi pooja,* it helps to cure mental illness permanently. Many people were being cured after coming to the temple with the blessing of Chottanikkara Amma (goddess).

The people believed that the cause's mental illness is the evil spirit, black magic, external fears, family issues, or exam fear. Moreover, they believe the condition is a lifelong problem because it is caused due to external forces. Once any human body comes across any evil or soul, it is challenging to save that human body from the evil/soul. The researcher found that the evil spirit usually leaves the body after attending the temple healing practices.

The researcher also recorded the patient's opinions and their family members about the allopathic treatment. Due to the firm superstitious and blind beliefs, people hesitate to consult the Allopathic medicine. They believe that Allopathic is not an appropriate treatment for mental illness, and it has many side effects. The continued medication causes health problems, and its allopathic medicine that is costly. Allopathic cannot make a cure for the illness, but it will make them tired due to its medications. It may lead to paralyzing the body. All of the researchers have no experience in Allopathic medicine because they do not use the medicines because they do not believe in Allopathic treatment. Most respondents consulted folk healers and indigenous medicine to heal their illnesses after the onset of illness.

In our society, the mental health field does not get proper attention to care; 20 million people have a mental illness, and the available services are minimal, especially in rural areas. The people have no adequate awareness of mental illness and its causes. Consequently, they consult traditional and indigenous healing practices for their illness. The research can give insight into the service situation and implement new programs for the welfare of the person with mental illness.

Implications of the Study

The mental health of the individual has been challenged since immemorial. As a branch of science, psychiatry has a long history and has gone through various interpretations of mental illness before it has reached today's approach. Though there are many studies in these specific areas; still, the present study will give more information in the field of medical anthropology, especially in mental health research.

The findings of this proposed study will help implement the new plans and programs and bring necessary changes to the existing ones. This empirical study helps get the beneficiaries' knowledge and their healing approach.

Future Scope for Research

Due to some constraints, the study focused on a limited sample size with a limited time. In the future, this study can be extended to a longitudinal study for accessing the impact of temple healing on the patients.

Dilemmas and Challenges Faced*:* The researchers faced several challenges during the data collection process that has elaborated on below;

1. Unwillingness to talk to the researcher: most patients are not interested in sharing their personal information. They feared that the data would out and may affect their future lives.
2. Language: In Chottanikkara temple, various people come for *Bajanam* (prayer) from Karnataka, Tamil Nadu, Andrapradesh, Bangalore, etc. Due to the language problem, the researcher couldn't be able to collect information from them other than Tamil and Malayalam.
3. Time constrains.

Recommendations for Social Work Interventions

According to the nature and complexity of mental illness, the symptoms vary significantly from one individual to another. It is heart-wrenching to see a loved one struggling with mental illness; most do not know how to help and support people with mental illness. The study recommends the following to be done to improve the situation of people with mental illness.

Conscientization campaigns should be conducted in rural areas to provide on mental health knowledge. They need to understand the early symptoms and acute symptoms of the disease. People need to know the warning signs of mental illness and seek proper assistance at the early stages of the disease—this need to be encouraged at the individual and community level.

Strengthen the understanding of mental illness among spiritual leaders. Since the study showed majority had a strong belief in temple healing, there is a need for the healers to know about mental illness issues. So, they can encourage their parents to properly adhere to medication or seek medical assistance even if they are receiving temple healing. Both can be very effective in helping people with mental illness. Temple healing is essential and must be strengthened since it provides patients with patience, hope, and calmness of mind from the belief that superior powers protect them.

Poverty also was highlighted among the causes for people to opt for temple healing. It means that some people wished to go for Allopathic medicine but failed to afford the expenses and went for temple healing after some time. This calls for particular intervention to improve the economic situation of the people. Because even if the government ensures the accessibility of modern health care, still people have no economic strength to access the services.

Lastly the Government and other stakeholders need to have a special eye on the health sector. The study showed that the resources allocated in the health sector are insufficient to meet the current situation. Much effort must

be invested in improving the quality of services. Accessibility and availability of mental health services should promote in rural areas to help people with mental illness.

Mental illness is a complex issue requiring diversified approaches and effective participation of various stakeholders to curb the problem. Individual initiative and readiness for people to care for their mental health is an obligation of everyone.

REFERENCES

Alter, J. S. (1999). Heaps of health, metaphysical fitness: Ayurveda and the ontology of good health in medical anthropology. Current Anthropology, 40(S1), S43-S66.

Banerjee, G., & Roy, S. (1998). Determinants of help-seeking behaviour of families of schizophrenic patients attending a teaching hospital in India: An indigenous explanatory model. International Journal of Social Psychiatry, 44(3), 199-214.

Benmebarek, Z. (2017). Psychiatric services in Algeria. BJPsych International, 14(1), 10-12.

Bhattacharya, K. C. (1954 [1931]). Swaraj in Ideas. Visvabharati Quarterly, 20, 103-114.

Biswal, R., Subudhi, C., & Acharya, S. K. (2017). Healers and healing practices of mental illness in India: The role of proposed eclectic healing model. Journal of Health Research and Reviews, 4(3), 89-95

Biswal, R., Subudhi, C., & Pathak, A. (2021). Beliefs on etiology and healing practices of mental illness among tribes in Eastern India. Mainstreaming the Marginalised: Fresh Perspectives on India's Tribal Story.

Bryman, A., & Burgess, B. (Eds.). (1994). Analyzing Qualitative Data (1st ed.). Routledge. https://doi.org/10.4324/9780203413081

Campion, J., & Bhugra, D. (1997). Experiences of religious healing in psychiatric patients in South India. Social Psychiatry and Psychiatric Epidemiology, 32(4), 215-221.

Charmaz, K. (1983). Loss of self: a fundamental form of suffering in the chronically ill. Sociology of health & illness, 5(2), 168–195. https://doi.org/10.1111/1467-9566.ep10491512

Collins, J., & Hussey, R. (2003). Business Research: a practical guide for undergraduate and postgraduate students. New York: Paigrave Macmillan.

Conrad, P. (1990). Qualitative research on chronic illness: a commentary on method and conceptual development. Social science & medicine, 30(11), 1257-1263.

Creswell, J. W. (2013). Qualitative Inquiry & Research Design: Choosing among Five Approaches (3rd ed.). Thousand Oaks, CA: SAGE.

Dein, S., & Illaiee, A. S. (2013). Jinn and mental health: Looking at jinn possession in modern psychiatric practice. The Psychiatrist, 37(9), 290–293. https://doi.org/10.1192/pb.bp.113.042721

Dube, K. G. (1970). A study of prevalence and biosocial variables in mental illness in a rural and an urban community in Uttar Pradesh—India. Acta Psychiatrica Scandinavica, 46(4), 327-359.

Dube, K. C., Kumar, N., & Dube, S. (1984). Long term course and outcome of the Agra cases in the International Pilot Study of Schizophrenia. Acta Psychiatrica Scandinavica, 70(2), 170-179.

Dhivya Dharsanam. (2008). Hanumanthapuram Sri Agora Veerabadhrar. Retrieved from http://www.dharsanam.com/2008/03/hanumanthapuram-agora-veerabadhrar.html

Dunn, F. L., & Janes, C. R. (1986). Introduction: medical anthropology and epidemiology. In Anthropology and epidemiology (pp. 3-34). Springer, Dordrecht.

Fiske, S. T. (2017). Prejudices in cultural contexts: Shared stereotypes (gender, age) versus variable stereotypes (race, ethnicity, religion). Perspectives on psychological science, 12(5), 791-799.

Flick, U. (2018). An introduction to qualitative research. Sage Publications Limited. Foster, G. M., & Anderson, B. G. (1978). Medical Anthropology. New York, NY: John Willey & Sons.

Foster, G. M., & Anderson, B. G. (1978). Medical anthropology. John Wiley & Sons, Inc.605 3rd Avenue, New York, NY 10016, USA.

Glick, L. (1967). Medicine as an ethnographic category: the Gimi of new Guinea highands.Ethnology 6, 31-56.

Hampton, N. Z., & Sharp, S. E. (2014). Shame-focused attitudes toward mental health problems: The role of gender and culture. Rehabilitation Counseling Bulletin, 57(3), 170-181.

Helman, C. (2007). Culture, health and illness (5th Eds). London: Hodder Arnold.

Hernandez, M., Nesman, T., Mowery, D., Acevedo-Polakovich, I. D., & Callejas, L. M. (2009). Cultural competence: a literature review and conceptual model for mental health services. Psychiatric services (Washington, D.C.), 60(8), 1046–1050. https://doi.org/10.1176/ps.2009.60.8.1046

Herrman, H., Saxena, S., Moodie, R. and Walker, L. (2005). Promoting mental health as apublic health priority. In H. Herrman, S. Saxena and R. Moodie (Eds.), Promotingmental health: Concepts, emerging evidence, practice (pp. 2–17). Geneva: World HealthOrganisation.

Kakar, S. (1985). Psychoanalysis and Religious Healing: Siblings or Strangers?. Journal of the American Academy of Religion, 53(4), 841-853.

Kakar, S. (1991). Shamans, mystics and doctors: A psychological inquiry into India and its healing traditions. University of Chicago Press.

Keyes, C. L. (2005). Mental illness and/or mental health? Investigating axioms of the complete state model of health. Journal of Consulting and Clinical Psychology, 73(3),539–548.

Kleinman, A. (1978). Concepts and a model for the comparison of medical systems ascultural systems.

Social Science & Medicine. Part B: Medical Anthropology, 12, 85-93.

Kleinman, A. (1980). Patients and healers in the context of culture: An exploration of the borderland between anthropology, medicine, and psychiatry. London: University of California Press.

Kothari, C.R. (2004) Research Methodology: Methods and Techniques. 2nd Edition, New Age International Publishers, New Delhi..

Kumar, D., & Subudhi, C. (2015). Reappraising disability in India: Model, magnitude, and measurement. *Journal of Disability Studies*, *1*(1), 23-30.

Kyziridis, T. C. (2005). Notes on the History of Schizophrenia. German Journal of Psychiatry, 8(3), 42–48

Mental Healthy (n.d.). Retrieved fromhttp://www.mentalhealthy.co.uk/general/general/what-mental-health.html

Miller G. E. (1990). The assessment of clinical skills/competence/performance. Academic medicine : journal of the Association of American Medical Colleges, 65(9 Suppl), S63–S67. https://doi.org/10.1097/00001888-199009000-00045

Ministry of Health and Family Welfare (MHFW) (2007). Annual report 2020-21. Government of India.

Murdock, G. P. (1980). Theories of illness: A world survey. University of Pittsburgh Pre.

Murthy, R.S. (2011). Mental health initiatives in India (1947-2010). The National medical journal of India, 24 2, 98-107 .

Ngubane, H. (1977). Body and mind in Zulu medicine; an ethnography of health and disease in Nyuswa-Zulu thought and practice.

Nguyen, D., & Bornheimer, L. A. (2014). Mental health service use types among Asian Americans with a psychiatric disorder: Considerations of culture and need. The journal of behavioral health services & research, 41(4), 520-528.

Nundy, S. & Desiraju, Keshav. & Nagral, Sanjay. (2018). Healers or predators? : healthcare corruption in India. New Delhi, India: Oxford University Press

OKely, J. (1994). Vicarious and sensory knowledge of chronology and change:ageing in rural France', in K. Hastrup and P. Hervick(eds) Social Experience and Anthropological knowledge.London: Routledge

Padmavati, R., Thara, R., & Corin, E. (2005). A qualitative study of religious practices by chronic mentally ill and their caregivers in South India. The International journal of social psychiatry, 51(2), 139–149. https://doi.org/10.1177/0020764005056761

Pathak, A., & Subudhi, C. (2020). Understanding psychological distress among female caregivers of the patients with mental illness. In Psycho-Social Perspectives on Mental Health and Well-Being (pp. 123-135). IGI Global.

Pillai, B. (2008). Greatness and glory of sree Chottanikara devi and the temple.

Raguram, R., Venkateswaran, A., Ramakrishna, J. and Weiss, M.G. (2002). Traditional community resources for mental health: A report of temple healing from India. British Medical Journal, 325(7354), 38–40.

Sadock, B.J., Kaplan, H.I. and Sadock, V.A. (2007) Kaplan & Sadock's Synopsis of Psychiatry: Behavioral Sciences/ Clinical Psychiatry. Lippincott Williams & Wilkins, Philadelphia.

Samuel, G. (2015). The contemporary mindfulness movement and the question of nonself. Transcultural psychiatry, 52(4), 485-500.

Satcher, D. (2001). Mental health: Culture, race and ethnicity. A supplement to mental health: are part of the surgeon general. U.S: Public Health service.

Satija, D. C., Singh, D., Nathawat, S. S., & Sharma, V. (1981). A psychiatric study of patients attending Mehandipur Balaji temple. Indian journal of psychiatry, 23(3), 247

Scheid, T.L. and Brown, T.N. (2010). Approaches to mental health and illness: Conflictingdefinitionsandvemphasis. In T.L. Scheid and T.N. Brown (Eds.), A handbook for the study of mental health: Social contexts, theories and systems (pp. 1–5). New York, NY: Cambridge University Press.

Scott, J., & Marshall, G. (Eds.) (2009). A dictionary of sociology. Oxford University Press. Indian Journal of Psychiatry, 19(4), 9

Sethi, B. B., Trivedi, J. K., & Sitholey, P. (1977). Traditional healing practices in psychiatry. Indian Journal of Psychiatry, 19(4), 9

Sinha, S. K., & Kaur, J. (2011). National mental health programme: Manpower development scheme of eleventh five-year plan. Indian journal of psychiatry, 53(3), 261.

Srivastava, V.K. (2002). Some thoughts on the anthropology of mental health and mental illness with special reference to India. Anthropos, 97(2), 529–541.

Stanford, M. S. (2007). Demon or disorder: A survey of attitudes toward mental illness in the Christian church. Mental Health, Religion and Culture, 10(5), 445-449.

Subudhi, C. (2014). Culture and mental illness. In Abraham F. et al., Social Work Practice in Mental Health: Cross-Cultural Perspectives, Allied publisher, India p. 132-140.

Subudhi, C. (2021). Beliefs about etiology, help-seeking and consequences of mental illness: A study on tribal patients from a psychiatric setup (Doctoral dissertation). National Institute of Technology Rourkela, India.

Subudhi, C., & Biswal, R. (2015). Mental health care services in India: An analysis of the mental health care bill 2013. *Int J Health Sci Res, 5*, 424-32.

Subudhi, C., & Biswal, R. (2020). Medical anthropology and epidemiology: a collaborative venture for mental health research in India. International Review of Psychiatry, 1-8.

Subudhi, C., Biswal, R., & Meenakshi, J. R. (2020). Healing preferences among tribal patient with mental illness in India. *Journal of Neurosciences in Rural Practice, 11*(02), 361-362.

Subudhi, C., Biswal, R., & Pathak, A. (2020). Willingness on hospital stay among the tribal patient with mental illness and their caregivers. *Journal of Psychosocial Rehabilitation and Mental Health, 7*(2), 183-187.

Subudhi, C., & Biswal, R. (2021). Perceived Beliefs about Etiology of Mental Illness among Tribal Patients in India. *National Journal of Professional Social Work*, 3-11.

Thara, R., Islam, A. and Padmavati, R. (1998). Beliefs about mental illness: A study of a rural south Indian community. International Journal of Mental Health, 17(3), 70–85.

Thompson, A.H. and Bland, R.C. (1995). Social dysfunction and mental illness in a community sample.v Canadian Journal of Psychiatry, 40(1), 15–20.

Trivedi, J. K., & Sethi, B. B. (1979). A psychiatric study of traditional healers in Lucknow city. Indian Journal of Psychiatry, 21, pp. 133-137.

Trivedi, J. K., & Sethi, B. B. (1980). Healing practices in psychiatric patients. Indian Journal of Psychiatry, 22(1), 111.

U.S. Department of Health and Human Services [USDHHS] (2001). Mental health: A report of the Surgeon General. Rockville, MD: Author.

Vallenga, J. (2008). Longing for health. A practice of religious healing and biomedicine compared. Journal of

Religion and Health, 47(3), 326–37. doi:10.1007/s10943-008-9175-0

Wang, P. S., Aguilar-Gaxiola, S., Alonso, J., Angermeyer, M. C., Borges, G., Bromet, E. J., ... & Wells, J. E. (2007). Use of mental health services for anxiety, mood, and substance disorders in 17 countries in the WHO world mental health surveys. The Lancet, 370(9590), 841-850.

Weiss, M. G., Sharma, S. D., Gaur, R. K., Sharma, J. S., Desai, A., & Doongaji, D. R. (1986). Traditional concepts of mental disorder among Indian psychiatric patients: preliminary report of work in progress. Social Science & Medicine, 23(4), 379-386.

World Health Organization (2001). Mental health: New understanding, new hope. WorldMentalvHealth Report, Geneva: World Health Organisation.

World Health Organization. (2005). Dept. of Mental Health, & Substance Abuse.(2005). Mental health atlas 2005. World Health Organization.

World Health Organization. (2006). The world health report 2006: working together for health. World Health Organization.

World Health Organisation (WHO). (2014). mental health: A state of well-being.

World Health Organisation [WHO]. [2019a]. Mental disorders. Retrieved from https://www.who.int/news-room/fact-sheets/detail/mental-disorders

World Health Organisation [WHO]. (2019b). 10 facts on mental health. Retrieved from https://www.who.int/news-room/facts-in-pictures/detail/mental-health

Young, A. (1976). Internalizing and externalizing medical belief systems: an Ethiopian example. Social Science and medicine, 78.

APPENDIX

Interview Schedule

Demographic Details of the patient

Name:
Sex:
Domicile: rural/urban/tribal
Marital status: unmarried/married/divorced/separated
If married: years of marriage
No of children's:
If separated/divorced: time since separated/divorced and mention reason
Working status: Govt./Pvt./Self employed
Income (monthly) patient
Family members:
Demographic Details of the Family Members

Opinion and Belief about the Illness

1) One set of illnesses/problem
2) What do you call your problem? Specify the name(local name)
3) In your opinion, what is the cause of this problem?
 a) By family members' opinion:
 b) By patient opinion
 c) Any other cause (if):
4) How did they come to know about the problem (logic behind their opinion)?
5) What is fear about the illness?
6) Has anyone in your family ever had a similar illness to you?

Opinion about the Healing Practices

1) How you came to know about this temple
2) For how many days have you been here
3) Explain your daily practices?
4) Is it the first time, you are coming to the temple? Yes/No

If No, how many times you have come?

What were your past experiences?

Why you came again?

5) What you are doing during the menstruation cycle (if female)

6) If some agent work will come at home, what they are doing?

7) What do you feel during Guruthipooja (one ritual performed by the temple daily) session?

8) Do you feel any change after coming here?

9) Describe all treatment/ healing practices from the onset of illness?

(Folk healing, other healing, biomedical/ (psychiatrist)

10. Opinion about bio-medical treatment?

a.) Do you face any financial problem for taking modern medicine?

11) Give your opinion about this temple healing?

Related to Their Daily Life

1) Who is staying with the patient always?
2) Where are they staying at night and other time? (Amount for paying)
3) For care givers, how he/she managing his/her daily life here?
4) What problems do you face in your family/ community due to this illness?
5) Is there any history regarding physical injury (or attempt to suicide) to her/him or any other .if yes explain
6) How do family members and neighbours react towards your illness?

Photo Gallery

Entrance of Chottanikkara Temple

Way to Keezhkavu Temple

Chottanikkara temple Pond

Sacred Trees

(All the photos have taken during study by CR)

About the Authors

Dr. Chittaranjan Subudhi is working as an Assistant Professor in the Department of Social Work, School of Social Sciences and Humanities, the Central University of Tamil Nadu (by an Act of Parliament) Thiruvarur, India. He has a Bachelor Degree in Commerce and a Master Degree in Social Work from the Utkal University of Odisha, India. He has completed his PhD in Mental Health from the Department of Humanities and Social Sciences, National Institute of Technology Rourkela, India. He has conducted research in various areas like Health and Mental Health, Medical Anthropology, Family and Child Welfare, Disability studies, and Tribal Health issues. He teaches Psychiatric Social Work, Working with Individuals and Communities, Qualitative Research, ICTs in Social Development and Health System Management. He has written many articles including conference papers and published in national and international reputed peer-reviewed journals. He has written many articles including conference papers and published in national and international reputed peer-reviewed journals including Elsevier, Springer, Sage, Routledge, Taylor & Francis, Web of Science and other SCOPUS indexed journals.

He has extensive professional experiences in university teaching; research consultancy; extensive fieldwork supervision, mentoring postgraduate students; conducting various soft skill training and professional development programmes; organised various national, international conferences. He is also associated with various National organizations and associations including the Indian Society of Professional Social Work (ISPSW). Now he is a member of Equal Opportunity Cell, Gender Sensitivity Cell, and Discipline Committee, Central University of Tamil Nadu, from 2018

Email: chittaranjan.subudhi@gmail.com

Soumya S B has completed her Master of Social Work from the Central University of Tamil Nadu, India. She hailed from Thiruvananthapuram in Kerala. She has completed her Bachelor's degree in Social Work from Little Flower Institute of Social Science and Health under Calicut University. She started her career as a Social Worker at Nirbhaya shelter home under the social justice department. After that, she joined World Vision India, a child protection project as a project coordinator. Through World Vision India, she got many chances to inter with the children of poor communities and became a part of their joy moment.

Email: soumyabeenasreekumar@gmail.com

Edness Rutta is a research scholar at the Central University of Tamil Nadu. She is a self-reliant and confident social worker who has a sound understanding of social work values and skills and exceptional client handling skills. Excellent counseling skills, advocacy skills, very familiar with students' issues, and so determined to improve the lives of the marginalized groups. She has been working with children in conflict with the law as, an HIV/AIDS home-based care, and youth counselor at Mbeya University of Science and Technology.

Email: ednesrutta@gmail.com

www.ingramcontent.com/pod-product-compliance
Lightning Source LLC
LaVergne TN
LVHW050324160826
845677LV00014B/3536

9788195468409